Don’t worry, you’re n[illegible]heard of Alex Meade either. If [illegible] word to describe himself, it would be i[illegible]scribable. After completing an apprenticeship in Retail Management in 2017 he went on to reach heights that man thought not possible…like starting a second one in a completely different industry. Winning the ‘Apprentice of the Year’ award isn’t something Alex can claim because he didn’t, which is quite impressive when you consider he had two opportunities. Having left the world of apprenticeships behind and now in full time employment, he decided to use his experiences as the foundation for his first literary endeavour.

Alex Meade

APPRENTIPS

20 Tips For Apprentices Based On My Experiences

AUSTIN MACAULEY PUBLISHERS™
LONDON • CAMBRIDGE • NEW YORK • SHARJAH

A CIP catalogue record for this title is available from the British Library.

ISBN 9781035806645 (Paperback)
ISBN 9781035806652 (ePub e-book)

www.austinmacauley.com

First Published 2023
Austin Macauley Publishers Ltd®
1 Canada Square
Canary Wharf
London
E14 5AA

'If you can fill the unforgiving minute
With sixty seconds' worth of distant run,
Yours is the Earth and everything that's in it,
And – which is more – you'll be a Man, my son!'

To my father, Steven.

To go from a word document to a tangible hard copy has certainly been an experience to say the least. However, I'd like to thank Austin Macauley Publishers because, without all of your support, *Apprentips* never would have seen the light of day. You took a chance on an unknown, first time author for which I will be forever grateful.

I'd also like to take the chance to thank my family for their continued support. While I may have been the one typing away on the keyboard, *Apprentips* felt very much like a team effort.

Table of Contents

Introduction

I'm not what you would call an extrovert. I've been described as an 'introvert but sociable' or 'someone who comes out of their shell once you get to know them', and I think both are true for the most part. I also try to be very careful with my choice of words in addition to when I use them. As a result, I'm not one who finds it naturally effortless to introduce myself or hold a conversation. It turns out the same applies when comprising an opening paragraph.

Anybody who has had the pleasure or misfortune of meeting me (their choice) will know I keep my dialogue relatively brief and to the point. These two principles are the foundation of the book. What you are holding in the palm of your hand is essentially me talking to you through the medium of literature. Which part of me your hand is on is up to you.

So, at the time of writing (early 2022), three events are unfolding: Putin decided to invade Ukraine, an actor slapped a comedian at the Oscars, and I'm currently working through my second apprenticeship. Now, as much as topics one and two are clearly more interesting, for now, let's talk about number three.

Many moons ago (2015), I began my first apprenticeship. For the purpose of GDPR and potential future defamation lawsuits, I'm not going to state where it was or mention any names of colleagues. All you need to know is I worked in the retail industry as a kitchen designer. It was 18 months long, and I passed – a dream outcome. Roughly two years later, and due to some 'interesting' career choices, I ended up working in the construction industry. In October 2020, I began my second apprenticeship, which should finish in January 2022 if all goes to plan.

Spoiler, it didn't. The deadline was extended to June 2022, with a line being drawn in the sand by March 2022. In other words, I didn't complete it. Not so much a perfect outcome, more of a shit show.

In both cases, I learnt many lessons. Some personal and others lean more towards the professional working side. Unfortunately, for you gossip fiends, you aren't reading my autobiography, so I will leave most of the personal stuff out and focus mainly on the lessons relating to the apprenticeships. However, before we get into the weeds, let me answer some questions you may already be asking.

Why did your second apprenticeship fail?

I was working in the wrong department from the beginning. I spent a whole year flagging the problem, and nobody listened. By the time the penny finally dropped, it was too late.

Why have you bothered writing?

Case studies – I believe it was 2017 when the first company I worked for asked if I would speak to the new cohort of apprentices at the organisation's headquarters. I agreed but wasn't given much in the way of purpose, structure or content. On the train up, I thought about what advice I could give the group. I didn't want to be generic, and I wanted it to be helpful. I started making notes and then wondered if there was a book of similar nature, but I couldn't find anything. As soon as I got off the train, I bought a pen and a paper pad and began scribbling away.

Later in the year, I gave a talk to three sets of classes at a school in Milton Keynes about apprenticeships. The topics in the presentation were based on the book I was drafting at the time. Mentally, I was taken aback by the reactions I received as I was speaking. They seemed surprised or shocked at what they were hearing. It was almost as if they had been told to consider such information for the first time.

Roughly three years later, my perception was ratified. I presented to 15–20 teachers about my ongoing apprenticeship in construction, and afterwards, there was a virtual Q&A due to COVID. The questions asked highlighted a lack of understanding and awareness of various aspects of apprenticeships. So, if schools and teachers cannot shed much light on the topic and, from what I can see, students cannot access much information online, who is guiding/helping them? Unfortunately, it seems to be very few.

Generations – Now I have reached the old and weary age of 24, I have begun to ponder on the mysticism of life. One such topic I question is how I can help others, and here is what I concluded. At 24, you would think I would be happy, but really, I'm not. I have my own personal problems, and let's be fair, we all have them to varying degrees but from a career perspective, I'm down in the dumps. I regret a lot of decisions, and I made many mistakes in my time. I wish I had done things differently, and through the lens of hindsight, I realised how I made a rod for my own back, which is mostly to blame for my current mental state. But why should it matter to you? I'm just a stranger.

From a broader perspective, those who have experienced the real world should pass on their tales/advice to future generations. It can help them avoid the same pitfalls, achieve success faster and suffer less misery along their journey. My view is hardly ground-breaking as it is near enough the basis of parenthood. However, I realised I amassed a bank of knowledge about apprenticeships which, as far as I am aware, has not been publicly shared before. Therefore, I believe it is beneficial to share with you the lessons I have accumulated over the years. They are predicated on my own regrets, downfalls, and mishaps, which I hope will help those embarking on the next phase of their life.

Curiosity – As mentioned, I've had such an idea since about 2017 and was inquisitive about what would happen if I brought it to life. I am already fully aware my work will be no Harry Potter or 50 Shades of Grey. As much as I have tried, making apprenticeships sound magical or kinky is tricky. One element in crafting these pages was to see what would happen. Would it get published? Sell a single copy? Be read by anybody other than myself?

'Since 2017…' – What's taken so long?

Easy, I was lazy and gave up far too many times. I went through cycles of motivation and then procrastination, so these pages have been on my laptop, gathering virtual dust on multiple occasions. I know what you are thinking and won't argue with you. I only have myself to blame. Feels quite good to get it off my chest, but it also sets the theme, honesty.

Will it just be a sales pitch for apprenticeships?

No, far from it. I mentioned that my first apprenticeship was in retail, and one aspect involved selling. Long story short, I was useless. Everybody around me could sell water to a drowning man. I couldn't sell him a life jacket. My first commission slip was £-3.84. No, there wasn't a typo. It was indeed a minus. So, suppose I was trying to sell you apprenticeships. In that case, there is a high chance it would result in you returning your copy, getting a refund, and being put off by the idea.

The more meaningful answer to your question is, honestly, I have no vested interest in your future choices. I get no money, benefits, or perks if you choose to follow in my footsteps. Okay, you could argue I received some money when you purchased *Apprentips*, but wonga was not my focus. You are an individual who is responsible for your own future, and what you do is your decision. All I am here to do is give you an honest opinion of what the world of apprenticeships is like. If anything, I strongly encourage you to research going to university and taking a gap year to get a well-rounded view of your options. I can only speak about what I did, but whether or not you become an apprentice makes no difference to me. All I care about is helping you in your decision-making process, so whatever answer you come to, you are content and believe it is the right choice.

Will you be reflecting on / talking about your own experiences the whole time?

No, I won't. I may sprinkle in a couple of references, but I am trying to avoid using anecdotes for the following reasons:

- Over the years, I have written numerous versions of *Apprentips*. I originally wrote the first few using my own stories to explain the advice I was putting forward. Jesus Christ, it was boring, and I wrote the bloody thing.
- I speculate you don't actually care too much about my personal encounters. How the lesson came to be is neither here nor there. I think you just want the crux of the matter.
- Including all the details of each story will just lengthen the book. The idea is for each 'Tip' to be short, sharp, and snappy. Ideally, a book you could read in a day or two.
- The majority of elements from my apprenticeships and yours will most likely be completely different. The course you are completing, where you work, who you work with and the industry, to name a few. Therefore, the specifics of my apprenticeships will be less relatable to yours. I struggled to rationalise the importance of telling you about concrete or CAD (Computer Aided Design) when you might be an aspiring chef, for example. Instead, I chose things that can be applied across most of the apprenticeship spectrum.

Wow, was there a shortage of paper or something?

I've somewhat explained why in the last section, but I'll expand. My rationale could be considered self-centred, or it might simply highlight the ignorance of my younger self. When I was growing up, I loathed reading because everything seemed to be so long and drawn out. In my opinion, many pages seemed to be fillers, and I believed books could be condensed; how naïve. It probably explains why I prefer to get to the point sooner rather than later instead of having superfluous conversations beforehand. My target audience is younger people, and I presumed they would also have a similar aversion to reading. I thought if I kept it 'short, sharp and snappy', it would be easier to read it in its entirety, and it won't feel like such a chore. I don't think asking you to read a few pages per chapter is really too much to ask.

Why are chapters called Tips?

Here is where I may expose how deeply I have been thinking. All I am doing is providing some advice based on my experiences. I originally called them 'Lessons' in the previous versions I wrote, but I felt it was too strong of a term. At the end of the day, I'm not telling you what you must do as a command; simply suggesting. Whether you act on such advice is up to you. Therefore 'Tip' seemed more apt.

What are you an expert in exactly?

At present, nothing. Throughout the book, I will mention factors such as feelings, emotions, thought processes and people's behaviour. For the record, I am no business guru, subject matter expert or psychologist. The following advice is based on my experiences, observations and reflection on my time as an apprentice. You may have your own reasons why you should behave in a certain way which differs from what you are reading. As I mentioned earlier, apprenticeships have many unique elements (and life in general), so one rule does not work for all. I'm not claiming what I have written should be gospel, just some advice for you to ponder.

"Well, what if…?"– Just for all of you, pedantic, finicky bunch.

Yes, I will make sweeping statements or some form of generalisation, all of which are based on my experiences. However, there are always situations where rules can be broken or do not apply. As the saying goes, 'For every rule, there is always an exception'. Now I think about it, even saying 'always' in the previous sentence, considering what I just said, was probably a mistake. Anyway, *Apprentips* would be a never-ending book if I had to cover every eventuality or possibility, so I have tried to be as accurate and truthful as possible considering the number of permutations there are in the world of apprenticeships and apprentices.

Keep these points in mind when you read each page. It's too easy to have a knee-jerk reaction to people's opinions. I wrote the following with all the best intentions and careful consideration.

Why is the word ‘this’ not in the book?

You probably wouldn’t have noticed unless I mentioned it. Anyway, my father would remind me to keep the number of times that word was included in my work to a minimum. It was one of his pet peeves about writing. Initially, a search via Word found it over 500 times. So as a small inside joke, I took his advice to the extreme and removed every mention of it from the following pages. So, aside from the paragraph’s title, excluding the copyright page, and the quote on page 96, it isn’t included. Go check; I’m not lying.

My mother then joked, “What about the word ‘that’?” and bloody hell, it was included 482 times! It looked like I had just done ‘find and replace’ and swapped one word for another. Anyway, the second word only appears 85 times. Personally, I don’t think that is too shabby.

I’m hoping all your questions have now been answered. Time to begin Tip 1.

Hold Your Horses

Well, before we get to Tip 1, perhaps we should quickly cover what an apprenticeship actually is and how it works.

The purpose

A very high-level definition I pinched from an online source is 'an apprenticeship is a paid job where the employee learns and gains valuable experiences' (apprenticeships.gov.uk), and surprise, surprise, they aren't wrong. However, I feel the definition is too high if you are searching for an accurate understanding of an apprenticeship.

Really what you are doing is constructing a sturdy foundation through learning, practising, and developing a set of skills over a defined duration. After your apprenticeship, you will build upon your foundation, regardless of your next career move. Some skills you will have already, and others will be completely new. For example, you will most likely have already practised, in some form, your communication, timekeeping and organising skills through your school 'career' and/or any work experience. Whether you were any good or not is another question. These will be developed further. In conjunction, you will then learn and practice new skills during the apprenticeship, such as using particular software, facilitating meetings, or operating machinery to pluck out a couple of random examples.

The result is a varied combination of skills you can use to develop in the role you might be offered if you pass. Alternatively, you may change career paths and some, if not all, can be transferred to your new area of work. Either way, your apprenticeship has still provided you with a set of skills.

In addition, you are opened up to a near-endless list of experiences. You meet new people and build your network, grow your character, maybe visit new places, create memories, impact a team or company, make a name for yourself, and to some degree, understand the world more. In 32 months (combining both apprenticeships), I learnt about designing, selling, carpentry, building materials, logistics, supply chain, construction, Lean, Six Sigma, innovation, recruitment, reporting and data analysis, in addition to developing the soft skills (for example, listening and communication). I only really realised how much I had learnt towards the end of my second apprenticeship when I was reflecting on my journey. Apprenticeships aren't so much a question of what you want to do or where you want to work. It is more appropriate to ask what skills you want to learn and develop.

I believe there is a misconception, or perhaps it is a stereotype, that apprenticeships are not really important. They may be viewed as a tick-box exercise for organisations due to the Apprenticeship Levy (I'll explain later) and not considered in the same league as university degrees or other qualifications. However, from my experience, they're essential and deserve to be taken as seriously as others. After all, as I just explained, it is setting the foundation of your career.

The structure

I'm in a slight pickle here because I want to explain how an apprenticeship works from a qualification standpoint, but I face a tiny issue called the Government. The Government, especially with education, seems to change its mind every other year. I did two apprenticeships, both of them with different formats. However, as of March 2022, here is how an apprenticeship works.

From what I understand, the Government introduced the 'Apprenticeship Levy' in 2017 to incentivise and support companies implementing apprenticeships. In short, it is a tax a company must pay if its total 'pay bill' is above £3 million per year. The tax is 0.5%, and they have 24 months to reinvest the money back into their company via apprenticeships; otherwise, all the contributions go into the coffers of the Government (probably only to be wasted). It is worth noting the company does not have to use the money just on younger people looking to take their first step on the career ladder. Instead, they may use it to upskill certain employees.

If your organisation does not meet the pay bill criteria, it does not have to pay into the Apprenticeship Levy. Instead, it pays 5% of the cost of the apprenticeship, with the Government topping up the remaining 95%. That sounds like a sweet deal to me.

Okay, so the background stuff probably won't affect you personally, but I think it is still useful to know. Anyway, moving on to elements that are more likely to.

As an apprentice, you are both working and studying simultaneously. Working on the day-to-day tasks set by your line manager and studying towards your qualification. Now it seems harsh to make you do both at the same time during your working hours, and the government agreed.

Apprenticeships include 'off-the-job training', which consists of 20% of your contracted working hours. Don't worry; you still get paid. The 20% is designed for you to receive some form of training, whether it be practical or theory-based. You might get to go somewhere with a team, attend a lecture workshop, or it may be used as the time when you focus solely on your apprenticeship coursework. How you set aside your mandated 20% can be done in two ways.

1. The company might have structured your course and worked it out for you. During my first apprenticeship, the organisation sent us all to its headquarters once a quarter for a week. There we received a variety of training. We even got a food and drinks allowance, and the hotel was decent…good times.
2. You discuss with your line manager how you incorporate the 20%. Such was the method for the second apprenticeship. My college lecture was every Wednesday, so Wednesday was chosen as my 'study day' (I always hated the name) as it made sense. I set an out-of-office email every Wednesday to make people aware and continued with my course.

You really want to get the format agreed upon and in place ASAP, or you end up juggling both work commitments and apprenticeship commitments, which will only get more challenging as time goes on.

There is a document called the Apprenticeship Standard. Every single apprenticeship must have one. It sets out the requirements, including what you should learn and how you are to be assessed.

As an apprentice, you will likely hear the term 'KSB' quite often, and the acronym stands for knowledge, skills, and behaviours. You must demonstrate these three sets of criteria throughout your apprenticeship as you will be assessed against them. Usually, the KSBs are broken down into modules (for example, K1 / S1 / B1) which relate to a specific element within the area of knowledge, skills, or behaviours. Your tutor should run you through these near the start of your course, and they can also be found in the aforementioned Apprenticeship Standard.

Math & English – Most will require a minimum qualification level in Math and English. If you already meet the requirements (and can provide proof via certification), then great, you're at the end of the road. If you don't, then you will also be required to pass a Math and English exam at the required level, but training should be provided to help.

Evidence – In order to tick the box for each module, you have to provide 'evidence'. Your training provider should explain what counts as evidence and how it can be uploaded. The key message here is you need to understand how your work ties into the apprenticeship and get into the mindset of capturing and uploading evidence regularly. It is difficult to do retrospectively, and I'm speaking from a lot of experience.

2 birds – In both apprenticeships, I was required to upload more than one piece of evidence per module, which sounds like more work. The good thing is one piece can be applied to multiple modules (B5 & S1, for example), so consider whether the evidence can kill two birds with one stone.

RLL – Also, I had to complete Reflective Learning Logs (RLL), although the name may vary between training providers. They are a weekly submission where you have to say what you covered over the week & what more you need to learn in relation to what you just stated. It's not extensive, a paragraph or two would suffice, but just like the evidence, I would get into a routine to complete them on a timely basis.

In the latter half of the apprenticeship, your training provider & you will begin to discuss the topic around your End Point Assessment (the pass or fail moment) and what is required to pass. You may have to start thinking about a project, bringing together the evidence submitted in the RLL into a work journal, revising for the exam or whatever the Apprenticeship Standard requires. I won't lie; it's hard work and 100x harder if you haven't been paying attention or keeping things in order. However, once the majority of your work is complete, then you can start a new discussion. The Gateway.

Gateway

Gateway is the training provider's/employer's way of checking you are ready for your End Point Assessment. It consists of showcasing the coursework you have put together and your knowledge. It basically asks the question, "You ready?" Assuming there are no significant issues, they can begin to organise the End Point Assessment (EPA), which is make or break time. It is worth noting the EPA cannot be undertaken until the Gateway assessment has been completed.

The End Point Assessment

An End Point Assessment is where you must demonstrate the KSBs to an independent person (unsurprisingly called an End Point Assessor) who has the final say regarding whether you have passed or failed. An End Point Assessor must be qualified to conduct the assessment and display continuous personal development in their given field. They will be knowledgeable & experienced, so it won't be any random person observing you. It also means you won't be able to blag your way through (it looks like the government thought of all loopholes).

Types of EPA – What you will be required to cover in your EPA varies between apprenticeships, but all will be explained in the Apprenticeship Standard. Below are the most common forms I have come across, but due to the wide variety of apprenticeships, it is possible there are others not on the list which are specific to your given industry. In most cases, completing more than one is required to pass your EPA.

- *Presentation* – A presentation about a project you completed as an apprentice. Usually, it will show a wide range of skills, application of knowledge and evidence of some behaviours. In the end, there will be a Q&A from the EPA to cover criteria they think may need a bit more evidence.
- *Exam* – In both cases, mine was multiple-choice, although after researching online, it looks like there

is an option of 'written' too. In my second one, I would have been allowed to take notes (I would double check if there is a possibility to do so with your training provider).

- *Professional Discussion* – You make a reflective journal/workbook to demonstrate the KSBs. The EPA will review it before the assessment, and then you have a recorded discussion about the workbook you submitted.
- *Practical assessment* – I never had one, but from what I understand, it comes into play when you have to show you have specific practical skills. For example, operating heavy machinery.

You will also be asked to bring somebody with you to the EPA who can validate the evidence you provided, confirm you didn't plagiarise anything, and that you actually did it. Most likely, it will be your manager. However, it is still worth clarifying as there may be flexibility for it to be somebody else.

There is a grading system of pass, merit or distinction, and the level you achieve depends on the quality of the evidence you have provided in the EPA. If you pass, then you will receive your certification. If you fail, the option is there for a retake. Although, you will need to discuss the possibility with your employer and training provider first.

Now, Sod's law will mean if *Apprentips* ever reaches the bookshelves of retailers, the second it does so, the government will decide it is now time to reveal the revamped apprenticeship format, and all of the above will be obsolete. So, there you go, a brief summary of how it all works.

Moving on to the first chapter, I promise.

Tip 1 – You

Before entering the minefield of job applications and coursework, we should focus on the most important person. You.

You may be in a position where you are too young to apply for an apprenticeship; in that case, you have the luxury of being able to consider the following before you take any action. However, others may be reading who are already applying or undertaking one. In that case, you may need a momentary break to complete the below.

You need to know who you are. It sounds ridiculous, but it is worth considering why. I didn't do it the first time around, nor the second. If you're holding my feet to the fire, I fell into both apprenticeships by sheer luck. I could have made better choices and focused on my career path rather than meandering aimlessly. Had I put real time and effort into my decisions, I may have avoided some stressful situations.

Why should you?

Realistically, you'll spend 33% of your day working. I based it on the assumption you will be/are working 9 am – 5 pm and do not have to stay late or work when you get home.

1/3 of your day isn't an insignificant amount of time. Do you really want to be doing something you don't like or doesn't excite you? I'm not saying every second of every day will stimulating, but you at least want to be in a place where getting out of bed in the morning isn't the worst thing in the world.

Criteria

Apprenticeships have criteria you need to fulfil, and these can be split into three types: Generic, knowledge & personal.

Generic – Strengths that everybody professes they are good at. Whether they are or not is another matter. Qualities such as timekeeping, being organised, being a good team player etc. I think these are perceived as 'tick box' qualities. It's great you have them, but they are somewhat expected and hardly something you can brag about.

Knowledge – Here can be a kick in your genitals, especially if you don't know what apprenticeship you want to do. You may find terms such as 'experience with…', 'Level 3 in…' or 'knowledge of….', and then it's followed by some specific software or qualification etc. Sometimes these can be deal breakers (known as 'must haves'). Other times they are viewed as 'preferable' or 'the ideal candidate will have'. It means the company is most likely only considering an individual who possesses such knowledge because it usually ties in with the apprenticeship. Not to say you shouldn't apply if you still want to, but your chances of being successful are reduced.

Personal – Now, here is what Tip 1 is really about. Personal traits are what make you, you. A marketing apprenticeship will most likely require an outgoing, creative, sociable individual with an interest in brands, advertising, and maybe even social media. A trade-based apprenticeship will need somebody with attention to detail as well as being dexterous. Day-to-day apprenticeship activities aren't the only things you need to consider. It's the type of team you will be working in, the ways of working and the organisation's culture. All require a variety of people with differing qualities. Whether you are that person or not, only you will know. You just don't want to permanently feel like an outsider because you cannot gel with everyone else.

While there may be some crossover between the two, you can see the significance of understanding and matching your attributes to those of the apprenticeships you are reading about.

T.I.M.W.O.O.D.S

The acronym relates to the eight types of waste you can find in an organisation. It is a principle of Lean, which you can research if you want, but it bears relevance because of the 'S'. The final letter stands for 'skills'. In an organisation, some people work in areas when they would be better suited elsewhere. You can match your skills to a particular role or industry by understanding yourself. As an apprentice, there are few things worse than having a good set of skills you cannot utilise, speaking from experience.

Interviews

You could get hit with vague questions like 'Tell us about yourself' or 'What are your strengths'; I think these questions are the worst for the following reason. You should know the answers immediately because they refer to you, yet they are the hardest to answer. Ums or pauses usually follow because nothing comes to mind straight away. I think the reason may be that you do not ponder the question very often, if at all. If I were to ask you a question about your partner, pet, or favourite sports team, you'd be able to reel off information until the cows come home (Jesus, I hope so for the first one…). Putting time aside to get to know yourself like the back of your hand is the easiest way to combat these dreaded interview moments.

If you don't know who you are, how will anybody else?

Tip 2 – Wine

The day I can uncork a bottle of red wine and actually enjoy it with a meal is when I will say I have reached true maturity and sophistication. Until then, and feel free to drink it yourself; I'm not sipping any bottle of grape garbage.

I only know three things about wine. First, it comes in three colours. You have to do a whole rigamarole to really taste it, including spitting it into a bucket. Finally, there is a strong connection between good wine and New Zealand. I don't know what the relationship is, but there is one, apparently.

Oh, actually, make it four. Certain wines go well with certain foods/meals. The technical term is 'pairs', but I'm no expert, so 'go well' will do for now. The skill of matching wine and food appears to be a fine art which requires all sorts of stuff, from whatever a 'good pallet' is to background knowledge of the wine itself. As it turns out, it's not just all about an eye-catching label and an eye-watering price tag.

Sommeliers (those with knowledge about wine to me and you) put a lot of time into researching the beverage to be sure they know what food pairs with what wine. If somebody spends a considerable amount of time and effort matching alcoholic grape juice to food, I think it is safe to assume you should do the same with your apprenticeship and you considering your career is far more important than some old plonk.

It turns out you can be an apprentice sommelier. Tad awkward now…

What to look for

Assuming you took my advice from the last chapter, you should now have (or plan to have) a more detailed insight into who you are. The question now becomes, what apprenticeship suits the real you? There are stereotypes such as an analytical mind should work with data, but there are now apprenticeships in nearly every field, so the world is your oyster. Look at what you are being offered and compare it to what you know about yourself. Maybe it's a match made in heaven, or perhaps you are polar opposites. Of course, not all elements will pair with what you know about yourself, but the big question with those is; do you view them as deal breakers or just minor inconveniences?

Happy – Well, when you think about it, does the job description make you so? Your mental wellbeing is far more important than people talk about. Your late teens/early twenties should be some of the happiest times of your life. I've already admitted that it is unlikely you will be happy every second of the working day, but if you're going to spend 33% of your time focusing on a subject, shouldn't you at least be satisfied and not miserable? It's funny how quickly you know whether something isn't right for you. If it isn't because you saw a glaring red flag, it is usually because of gut instinct, and such feelings are tough to overrule. Obviously, consider carefully what you are reading without jumping off the cliff of conclusion too quickly, but at the end of the day, you know yourself better than anybody. A good test is to attempt to explain why you do not want to continue with the option. 'I'm just not feeling it' isn't a good reason as there is one, it may just be deep inside. Explaining why can help narrow your field of vision and make the shortlisting process easier.

First impressions – You actually get a snapshot of your potential employer before they see you. It doesn't hurt to do some high-level research before you apply. Checking out the company on Google won't tell you everything. However, you might be able to envisage the type of culture, working style and people you would be engaging with. I thought of applying in a few cases, but after digging around, I realised it may be best if I didn't. It's not always to say the company is at fault. It could just be you didn't think your 'personalities' would pair well together.

Deal breakers – While you may be open to new ideas, it also helps to know what you are not prepared to commit to. There are endless reasons why you may not choose to apply, but knowing these before looking can make the filtering process easier. For example, you may have a minimum salary requirement due to personal expenses. Perhaps you don't drive, so what you define as a reasonable commuting distance may be limited. Maybe it is for ethical or environmental reasons. The point is, know where you draw the line, and you can look out for these when browsing job descriptions.

Red flags – Not to say every job description or organisation has these, but it is still worth keeping an eye out for. Unfortunately, there are some people who see apprenticeships as cheap labour but mask it as something else to reel you in. I'm not naming names, but there are a few bad apples you may come across in the barrel of apprenticeships.

Decision Making

Gravity – Sometimes you just happen to fall into things by chance. I did with my two apprenticeships, and I was extremely fortunate. I don't recommend you make falling your primary method of deciding on your future (remember I didn't utilise Tip 1) because it is risky. Occasionally, you might encounter an intriguing opportunity you hadn't previously considered. It might not be a job description but a social media post about something, an article or even a YouTube video. Who knows where going down these avenues may lead? Call it what you want, chance, fate, or God's plan but life has a funny way of working out sometimes. Unless you are dead set on something specific, there is no harm in keeping your mind open & exploring new possibilities.

Miscalculations – You may not get it right, and there is no guarantee you will be cock-a-hoop with the apprenticeship you end up in. It's all about probability at the end of the day. Consider the below.

Elements of the job description, findings via research and first impressions of the company (and later on interviews) – all have weight. These can be placed on either side of a scale, the positive side or the negative side. The weight of each one depends on how much you value the specific factor. For example, one positive might outweigh three negatives.

Every step you progress in the job application process gives you more things to consider. Company culture, the team you will be working with, hours expected etc. The question now is, once you have placed everything on the relative sides, is the scale more positive than negative? I know people who have rejected job offers because they were told they had to work weekends. Was it the right thing to do? Maybe for them, but it shows how working weekends or the expected hours carried far more weight than commute distance or potential salary. Nobody can be 100% certain their apprenticeship will work out as planned or even at all. In my first, several people dropped out, and I didn't complete my second.

I hope the above-made sense because trying to come up with a terse and coherent explanation was harder than I first thought.

Eternity – I used to try and picture the next 20 years of my life at the prospective employer, but why? It is illogical. It won't be your forever job, so there is no need to look at it as such. There is a lot of pressure placed on teenagers to get their career sorted early. I recommend not to look through the lens of 'Can I see myself working here or in the industry for the next couple of decades?' but rather 'Would I enjoy working there for the duration of the course?' as that is all you are contracted to do. I'm not saying you must get it right, or having the option to leave/resign/quit should mean you are lax with your choices. I'm simply advising that it helps to make such considerations now so you can avoid as much potential pain and suffering as possible in the future.

I highly recommend putting some time aside to make sure you and your job pair well together; otherwise, you may find your choice ages like milk rather than fine wine.

Tip 3 – Rollercoasters

I hated them, but now I love them. However, Tip 3 isn't about those adrenaline-inducing rides. It is the journey you go through when applying. It is full of ups and downs, butterflies in your stomach, and sometimes, you may feel like you are going backwards rather than forwards.

I don't think it would be too outrageous to claim that the education system predominantly focuses more on getting students to university than on apprenticeships. From the perspective of the school, therc is good reason to do so. There is a societal belief those with university degrees, on average, are more successful. In addition, parents (should) want their kids to have the best possible start in their careers. Therefore, in theory, it requires their child to obtain a degree. If a school can state a high percentage of their students are going to university each year, it is an indicator to the parents of how good the school is. As a result, the school attracts more pupils, possibly more funding, and the cycle continues. Every year, on results day, the news always talks about university acceptance rates and ushers people on the television or radio to give help and advice. However, as justified as it may seem, such rationale casts a bright light over those who want to attend university but leaves the rest in the dark, holding a candle.

I finished school with average A-Levels. For those curious, I did Biology, History and Religious Studies. I think the mix of subjects proves just how little thought I put into my future career. However, I knew I didn't want to go to university. Partly because I was too damn lazy, so didn't bother to do the research. Also, I didn't know what I wanted to do with my life, so why fork out a whole load of money? The latter was also a result of not bothering to complete Tip 1 myself. Therefore, an apprenticeship seemed like the next logical step. However, securing one was a lot harder than I first thought. Below are the things I wish I had known well before I began applying.

Suits – Well, there is nothing quite like reinforcing a point. I explained in Tip 1 and Tip 2, you need to know who you truly are. It will help you understand which potential apprenticeships are likely to be a good match for you. Read the job description carefully and see if your positive attributes match their ideal candidate. If so, brilliant. If not, then you have to think realistically. Is it suitable for you, and do you realistically have a chance of getting the job with your current skill set? Not to say you shouldn't still apply. More a case of, currently, are the scales tipped in your favour?

Fun fact: I once applied for a job at a well-known French sandwich shop and, sacrebleu! I was rejected within eight minutes of sending in my online application. It sucked, but realistically, I didn't have the relevant skills they wanted. I never stood a chance. However, I did learn a valuable lesson.

Detectives – It is time to research now you have a final filtered list of potential apprenticeships. Not only can your information gathering help with your cover letter and CV, but also with the interview stages because they will ask you questions, and lots of them. Obviously, with questions come answers, which you need to know. Essentially, find out every bit of information possible, whether it is about their products, company history, finances, employee reviews (go on glassdoor.co.uk), visit a store or workplace (if possible), take leaflets, subscribe to newsletters, the list goes on and on. Knowledge is never wasted.

Generic – You don't just have one CV. Once you have made one, what you possess is the foundation for every single CV you are going to send. It should always be adapted/updated for the job. Every job is different, which means every CV should be too. The same applies to cover letters. Your CV is the company's first impression of you, so you must show you have everything (or at least the majority) of what they have asked for. What have you done in the past or doing currently that ties in with what they are asking for? How can you show you have the skill set they are requesting? What characteristics have you got that match their ideal candidate? It does take time to personalise the document, but it can significantly increase your chances of getting to the next step. The same applies to cover letters too.

- Keep your CV brief, two pages max. Cover letters, one-page max. Recruiters are busy and don't want to be sifting through page after page. They just want the details upfront.
- KISS: An acronym for 'Keep It Simple, Stupid'. It's not an art assignment. No need for pretty pictures of

you or vibrant colours. A simple Word document, in most cases, will suffice.

- Don't lie. I did once. It nearly came back to bite me. I said I was learning sign language, which technically was true if you count one 10-minute lesson from a friend as learning. The topic came up in an interview, and somehow, they only expressed surprise I was learning such a skill and moved on. Had they asked a single question, I would have been up a certain creek without a paddle. So yeah, truth only.

Button basher – You may have apps on your phone where you can apply through various sites but be careful. You upload your CV, and then whenever you see a job you like, you just click a button and job done, right? As you would guess, no. I tried, and it did not work at all. Wherever I was (train, home, car journey but only as a passenger, obviously), I would open the app and then spend the next half an hour just clicking the 'apply now' button for various jobs. It was so easy to apply, and I took full advantage. In reality, I was wasting my time. I never changed the CV to suit the job, didn't read the advertisement properly to see if it suited my skill set, no research, and also no record keeping of what I had applied for. Although I thought I was being productive, I was actually being a very busy fool. Applying for two jobs properly will be more effective and better for you than randomly applying for twenty.

Hoops – Holy crap, you might have to jump through a load of hoops with some companies. You can get lucky; they will just ask for a CV and cover letter. Others want to know your entire life history (figuratively speaking), answer vague questions about yourself and then complete some assessments. It's a pain in the arse, but sometimes you have to accept it is going to take a while and crack on.

Interviews And Assessment Centres

Probably the part people dread most when it comes to the recruitment process. Understandable when you consider you have a make-or-break opportunity. A small window of time in which you have to show you are the right person out of a pool of candidates who tick most, if not all, of the requirement boxes too.

Prepare – Chances are you will be nervous on the day, so you want to alleviate any unnecessary stress in your life. The day before: Get all your clothes ready, set three alarms so you can't oversleep, collect any documentation (passport, CV, qualifications etc), know where your bag, money and keys are, fill up with petrol or get your train ticket in advance, plan your journey so you know how long it will take and then leave with time to spare, save the number of the point of contact for the company so you can get hold of them should you need to for any unforeseen circumstance. Preparation will make your life easier and help you stay as relaxed as possible. Remember, first impressions count. You not being in the chair when the time comes is one hell of a first impression. Better to be sitting in a waiting room for 30 minutes than to arrive just in time (or late) in a hot sweat.

- I just want to stress you need to keep hold of your certificates. Some companies require you to scan them into their system, while others may want you to bring the original copies as proof. While you may want to burn them because you hated the subject(s), don't. Keep them somewhere safe, as it's likely you will need them again. I actually have no idea if people burn their certificates, but it highlights my point.

Read – You might get sent a PDF or letter with instructions about the interview/assessment day. Read it carefully, and if something doesn't make sense, then contact them. Once, I contacted the company, and it turned out there was a mistake in the email. So you might be right in your concern, or you may be wrong, but you're better to be safe than sorry.

Dress code – A tricky topic for two reasons. First, I'm a man who is consciously aware women could be reading, and my knowledge of what constitutes appropriate female attire is virtually non-existent. To be honest, I don't care much for male fashion, either. The second reason is that every company is different, so I cannot apply a blanket statement, such as wearing a suit. My overall piece of advice is to check any emails/letters you have been sent. If you don't have somebody you can ask, try looking online for an answer, as someone may have written some advice that gives you an indication. If all else fails and you are unsure, contact the company/recruiter and ask. It may sound stupid, but it has its relevance. Being overdressed is not too bad, but being underdressed is something you want to avoid altogether.

Knowledge is key – The last point from 'Detectives' is crucial. Why do I stress researching so much? The first question I was asked during my first apprenticeship interview was, "What do you know about the company?" Research as much as possible because you never know what information you will need to have at your disposal.

Take your time – You don't have to say or do the first thing that comes to mind. Think before you speak or act. I'm trying to avoid using numerous clichés throughout each Tip (let's be honest, I failed spectacularly) but think of your behaviour as a tube of toothpaste. It's effortless to get the contents out of the tube. However, once it is out, it's bloody difficult to put it back, and you will probably make a mess in the process. I didn't come up with the toothpaste analogy, so credit to whoever did.

Questions – Think of some questions you would like to ask beforehand. You often get presented with an opportunity to at the end. It shows the interviewers you have given careful thought and consideration to your apprenticeship and the company. Ideally, ask things such as 'How much do I get paid?' or 'How many smoking breaks do I get?' Be creative and use some of the knowledge you have acquired.

Analysis – Avoid letting the interview play with your mind too much while waiting for the results. Whether you think it went well, disastrously, or indifferent, the result won't change. If it is a yes, then brilliant! If you receive a no, think briefly about what lessons you could take from your experience and move on to the next one. Maybe you know you bombed. Alternatively, you may have done nothing wrong, and somebody else on the day was better suited for the role. The outcome isn't dependent on how much you worry, so do whatever you usually do to relieve stress and relax.

Light at the end of the tunnel – I went through a period where I gave up applying. Every time I tried, I failed for various reasons. I missed the window of opportunity, I got halfway through applying and backed out, I got rejected or never heard back. All of these negative outcomes started to affect me mentally. However, I ended up being successful in one I never thought I would get. I did suit their requirements, but I still thought people would be better suited for it than myself. You will secure one at some point, I promise. It is just a combination of 'working smarter, not harder', staying positive, combined with a little bit of luck. Giving up makes everything more complicated and is not worth even thinking about.

Securing an apprenticeship is a bit of a rollercoaster ride, but it can be over much quicker than you think.

Tip 4 – Puzzles

Maybe you loved the educational aspect of school, or maybe you loathed it. Regardless, education will never go away, and the saying 'every day's a school day' holds weight, especially for apprentices.

"When am I ever going to need to know that?" is a common question students will often think to themselves when learning about a subject that they perceive to be pointless. Other smart-arse pupils directly asked their teacher. I wasn't the latter, but I was undoubtedly the former. The bizarre thing about life is, somehow, the majority of what you experience is all connected. Yet, you won't see it all come together until some point in the future.

Stick with me. The following analogy was the best way I could put my explanation across.

I think everybody is told, when completing a puzzle, to find the corner pieces and then the edge pieces to make the border. The early years of your life provide you with the corner pieces and a few of the edge pieces, which might not all be connected. By the end of school, you have a rough border at best. But your border, like the universe, from what I understand, is continually expanding. As you get older, so does the rate of expansion of your puzzle because you are exposed to more things you don't know about. What's worse, you don't even know what the picture of the puzzle is supposed to be, it can change rapidly (a life-changing circumstance), and yet, you have to make all the pieces fit. Confused?

Okay, for example, between the ages of 16–18, you become exposed to taxes, job applications, relationships, drinking, driving, insurance, gambling, politics, rent/mortgages and perhaps even parenting. All of which you know nearly nothing about in the grand scheme of things. You may understand some of the fundamental elements, but more doors have now been opened than ever before. There are more unknowns than knowns, and you have no idea what the impact on your life will be when looking into these new experiences. It also explains why you don't know what picture the puzzle is trying to convey.

So, your border is expanding. When you experience something new, life chucks at you a couple of pieces. Because you have little/no prior knowledge of the situation, you basically smush the pieces together and hope they fit correctly (known as trial and error). Mainly because, as I said, you don't know what the image is supposed to be. Therefore, you have no idea how they should fit, so you make your attempt. Then somebody (usually older and more experienced but not always) comes over and says, 'No, you idiot, you've done it wrong, it's like that,' and moves the pieces around to match correctly. Only then do you see how it should be. Maybe they move one piece, or they rearrange the whole thing. Either way, you now have a bit of your ever-expanding puzzle completed (an incredibly small percentage).

In some cases, you might have figured it out for yourself, or maybe you got it right the first time. The point here is it is trial and error for the majority of your attempts. However, now you know how the pieces are linked correctly, you should be able to repeat whatever you were doing with much more accuracy.

When you ask a question or do some further reading, life throws you a few more pieces because you now have some more information to hand. You might connect them all correctly, or you may have to try the smush technique again, but either way, you are increasing your piece count. Here is why educating yourself is so important. Your piece count needs to keep up as close as possible to the rate of expansion. If it doesn't, you begin to fall behind from an apprenticeship standpoint and life in general.

Eventually, you end up with groups of pieces dotted around your border. For ease, I will refer to these as islands. Islands form a relatively detailed image for those areas of your puzzle. It may be 10, 20 or even 50 pieces. There are others which are only still two pieces, and these are things you don't like working on or aren't interested in, hence why your knowledge and competency are low in these fields. Eventually, a few of these islands click together due to an event. For example, I hated learning about calculating areas in maths. So I ignored it, and then I ended up selling flooring as part of my job, where I had to manually calculate the areas of a room. You can imagine my joy when I realised. As your apprenticeship continues, more islands will join together as you make sense of your qualification, role & organisation. By the end, you will have a relatively big chunk of your puzzle completed as you have (fingers crossed) passed your apprenticeship. However, life continues, and so does the process. The act of gathering pieces and islands joining together is happening all the time because there is always something new to learn, more to understand, mistakes to be made, situations to encounter, crossroads to decide on, and lessons to be learnt.

You will never have a complete puzzle because you will never know everything. You may think my analogy is bloody awful, which is fair enough. But I am trying to show you that by educating yourself, you can make much more sense of what is happening around you. You can rely on others if you want to, but I wouldn't recommend it. You won't get as many pieces; chances are, all you will be left with is a vast border with very little inside.

The late great Steve Jobs once made a speech about 'connecting the dots' (you can find it on YouTube), and it is all about how things seem to be connected. It might not be now, tomorrow, or even a year, but eventually, all the knowledge you flippantly dismissed will become relevant.

In the workplace, knowledge is power, and life is a puzzle. It's up to you to retrieve the pieces.

Tip 5 – Spiders

We all have our phobias; as the title suggests, spiders are one of mine. I understand they have their place in the food chain/nature and 'they are more afraid of you than you are of them,' but those eight-legged bastards are creepy and unpredictable. The fact they are nocturnal is just the cherry on top of the web. I've become better with them over time, but by no means would I say they no longer bother me. Give me a snake or scorpion any day.

However, I think we all have a phobia, and nobody, at least in my career thus far, has ever spoken about it openly with me. It is the fear of failure. I'm sure you could find many influential motivational, or successful people who have discussed the topic, so by no means think I believe I am the pioneer of the subject. However, where there is work, there are mistakes, and breaking stigmas around it is important.

First things first

Natural – It's natural to be afraid of failing. Who wants to make a mistake and then live with the consequences afterwards? Nobody, right? We have to right our wrongs, answer to others, mentally process what happened (which can be difficult), and frankly, it can be embarrassing. Yes, there are scales in the severity of failure, but regardless nobody hopes to fail.

Accept – So I'll just say it, you're going to mess up on many occasions for various reasons, and once in a while, you're going to royally screw things up. Just ask those of an older generation, and I bet they all have at least one horror story, me included. Unfortunately, workplaces often expect perfection a lot of the time and don't take too well to the admittance of errors. However, we are all only human and far from perfect, so expectations and reality are often not the same. I believe you need to accept that failures will occur. If you don't, when the time comes, you will beat yourself up about it to the point where it can be detrimental. You can become apprehensive about learning or trying new things, seizing opportunities, and developing your character. You will stay forever in your comfort zone. I'm not proud to admit that the last lines came from experience.

Phase 1 – Types of failure/mistakes

Stupidity – Let's get the worst out of the way. The one where you know you messed up. You have no excuses. You can't blame anything or anyone, you just weren't thinking, and now a substance has hit the fan. A great example is losing the keys to the store when you are responsible for opening up. Who in their right mind would possibly lose store keys…I don't know…nope…not me…what an idiot…

It is a good idea if you can limit these to a bare minimum. The solution is to concentrate on what you're doing.

Learning – When you are first exposed to something new and try but don't quite hit the mark. You'll get some constructive criticism back; sometimes, you know you were awful. However, you're an apprentice. The only way to get better is to practice. You could debate whether it is viewed as failing but you're the reader, so you can decide for yourself. A saying I heard recently was 'to be the master first, you have to be the fool', and such a statement cannot be argued. You must accept you might 'fail' at first when trying something new otherwise, as I just said, you will never attempt to develop a wider set of skills or knowledge, which is really the essence of being an apprentice. You are locking doors closed before you have tried to open them (and not getting those puzzle pieces).

Good intentions – You try to be helpful, but there are unforeseen consequences. One instance is taking on too much work and promising more than you can deliver. While you intended to help with all thc goodwill in the world, it's more of a hindrance. Like many mistakes, people do not often see it from your perspective. Occasionally, not helping is better than offering.

Stress – Events pile up, and too many straws are placed on the camel's back. It's in the moment when you aren't in control of your emotions, and you say things or act in a way you shouldn't. Now, others will say, 'Don't get stressed', 'Never shout', 'Just grit your teeth and bare it', but the reality is everybody gets stressed. So yes, you may sometimes lose control and do/say something you shouldn't have. My advice is to understand your symptoms of stress so you can act on them early (basically Tip 1). I'm not saying in doing so, you will stop the build-up of stress in its entirety, but it's still an essential skill to learn. Take a break, rant to a friend, write it down, play sports or whatever you need to do to lower your blood pressure (ideally not at the expense of your apprenticeship, obviously).

Phase 2 – Dealing with it

So, phase one is over. Let's look at phase two, which is the more important part. What to do when you have an 'oh shit' moment. There are two parts, each of which you need to consider.

Imagination – So you messed up. Let's be fair; you're probably thinking the worst. Your manager will be livid, you will lose your job, you'll have no money, and the list goes on. However, most of these potential consequences are based on no evidence at all. I imagine you are in a sort of 'fight or flight mode' due to some biological evolutionary mechanism. Now there are mistakes, and then there are *mistakes*, but in both cases, you need to develop some form of control for your initial panic-like response.

How? Honestly, just get on with it. Speak to whoever you need to and tell them. If you have a solution, bring it up in conversation. It is far better to bring it to the colleague's / manager's attention than the other way around, especially if you knew about it. Plus, time is of the essence, so waiting can actually make things worse. Sitting and festering about your mistake does not help. Knowing things are out in the open plus a solution is being implemented takes a massive weight off your mind. It takes guts to raise the alarm, but overall, it's for the best. Oh yeah, be honest too. None of the 'dog ate my homework' nonsense.

What mistakes do is disrupt your plan. You did A, and rather than getting B, you got C. Now you don't know what to do because the output didn't match what you expected. As you didn't plan for the outcome, you also didn't plan for the consequences of said output, and you don't know what these are, which leads to the imagination element. As mentioned, you're probably imagining various outcomes, but you have no idea what will happen next or what your boss or customer will say. I discovered that it is usually never as bad as you expect. Even when I really screwed up, the consequences were never as dire as I assumed. Of course, people's emotions quickly take over. Words can be exchanged, which isn't pleasant, but after a while, people remember you're learning. A quick chat over a coffee, and the error is water under the bridge. Unless you lose the store keys, it's a bit different…a friend once told me…

Reality – A positive: it's highly unlikely you have shut the company down. You're an apprentice, not CEO. In the grand scheme of things, your mistake isn't catastrophic. It's tricky to dissect mistakes because the category is so broad and varied. However, as an apprentice, yours will have something in common. They can be fixed. It might involve getting a bit embarrassed in the short term or maybe doing some hard graft, but a solution can be found. I know because, when it comes to mistakes, I've been there more times than I want to admit.

Aftermath

Idiot – Don't be one and keep repeating the same error. Learn from it. People are willing to help until they realise you aren't helping yourself. Take some time to determine why you messed up, what the true cause was and what you could have done differently. Again, I find the solution in most cases is to concentrate or better preparation.

Dwell – Okay, somewhat counter-intuitive, but once you have thought about it and taken away the lessons learnt, try to forget about the event. I don't mean literally, as it is near impossible, but try not to become fixated. I mentioned earlier about 'beating yourself up', and you can become trapped in a nasty cycle which is tough to break. Mainly because you aren't thinking clearly, you make more mistakes, which further adds to your catalogue of errors you are already fixated on. Accept you weren't perfect, promise yourself you won't repeat the action again, and occupy your mind with something else.

Stick – You will get some. People laugh at others' misfortune, so take it gracefully and go along with the banter. Remember, it's a two-way street. You can give as good as you get if you have quick wit and the right type of working relationship.

I tried structuring these chapters to create a coherent flow rather than jumping from topic to topic. However, after finishing Tip 5, I recommend you go back and read Tip 4 as it may put some things into more perspective, just a suggestion.

So, when it comes to failure, just like when you find a spider, you need to learn how to deal with it because an encounter is inevitable.

Tip 6 – High Jump

Dick Fosbury, what a legend. Mr Fosbury changed a sport forever. Every professional high jumper uses his technique.

'Prior to the Games, the dominant high jump technique was the 'straddle'. Fosbury had not had much success…in fact as a high school athlete, Fosbury had failed to even qualify for his local club team in the high jump event. But instead of giving up, in 1963 Fosbury began working on a new jumping technique that would change the way athletes approached the sport from that time onwards. It came to be known as the Fosbury Flop.' – *Olympics.com*

Fosbury himself, on the revolutionary technique, said, "I believe that the flop was a natural style and I was just the first to find it." – *Olympics.com*

What's the Fosbury Flop got to do with apprenticeships? Well, he wasn't afraid to do things his way, and neither should you.

I think there is a big problem with the current education system. Unfortunately, it looks like it isn't going to change anytime soon. First off, you spend an average of nine years in an environment which should have been designed to prepare you for adulthood. Yet, for some unknown reason, schools do not teach you the life lessons you need to know, such as taxes, mortgages, insurance, avoiding/managing debts, having a happy, healthy, strong relationship, genuine discussions on drugs and alcohol, pregnancy, and abortions, cooking basic meals (not all schools granted) or even basics like how to hang up a picture or assemble furniture using basic tools. However, I personally believe schools limit your creativity and your way of thinking, which is what Tip 6 is about. As students progress through the education system, they lose their imagination or become too afraid to suggest something new or try something different. Rather than being able to think outside the box, your creativity dies and stays trapped inside. I suppose 'the box' becomes a coffin.

Everybody is different – What is fantastic about being an individual is how your life is unique. Nobody has had the same life you have. Your brain is wired differently. You see the world from a different perspective. You are an individual and you have your own ways of learning and working. Chances are, what works for you might not work for somebody else. You should embrace your uniqueness.

Listen to others – As an apprentice, it is almost certain you will be the least experienced and near enough one of the youngest people in the organisation. Therefore, everybody else around you is older, wiser, and more experienced with the processes and workings of the company. Therefore, it would be stupid not to listen to them and take on board what they are saying when they are taking the time to explain. However, you may not get told the same method(s) or advice by every individual. At the end of the day, they will also have their own ways. For example, some prefer phone calls and others like email. Some have routines and patterns, while others are less regimented. Some follow company policy to the letter, and some circumvent the rules. Who and why you listen to somebody is your choice, but it would be crazy not to utilise the wealth of knowledge surrounding you.

Experiment – You are there to learn, and one way is through trial and error, as previously discussed. Copy somebody for a bit and see if it works for you. Cherry-pick traits from individuals you think can be replicated. Maybe you form a hybrid working system based on what each person has told you. Alternatively, go full Fosbury and create your own new and unique way. The point here is, don't be afraid to experiment and discover a method of working that suits you. We are humans, not robots. I fell into the trap of copying the most successful person in the room and being adamant it was how I should work. The real issue was I wasn't them. My preferences did not match their operating model. No wonder I was terrible at sales.

Be confident – More on self-belief later but believe in yourself! If you're happy with how you do things, then have some confidence when explaining or showing others.

Arrogance – Sometimes, you will be doing something your way, and somebody will question why you have chosen to do it as such. Three things to note:

1. Try not to throw up a defensive barrier (as tricky as it may be) because somebody is critiquing you. It is more likely they are just trying to be friendly and save you time and /or injury.
2. Listen to others. They might have a valid point.
3. Explain. It's a chance for both of you to learn. Nobody benefits if one or both become defensive and argumentative (let's face it, who wants to be wrong).

Not to say you have to do what they say as, again, you are an individual, but who knows, they might be right.

Legality – Earlier, I said 'circumvent the rules' and we have arrived at a rather grey area. Companies have their processes and policies in place for a reason. These have evolved over time to maximise productivity, incorporate new software, apply the lessons learnt from past mistakes, or mitigate corrupt behaviour. The steps in a process should be arranged so that as many mistakes as possible can be avoided because these can result in a loss of money, time, reputation, and customers. The organisation expects you to follow these, and any breaking of the rules, depending on the severity and impact, can lead to various consequences. However, where there are humans, there is ingenuity. Ingenuity leads to new ways of working which don't match current processes and policies. See the problem? The question now is, should you utilise the unregulated method regardless of how you know of it?

The benefits – Do you save a bit of time? Maybe you should. Do you make money illicitly through a loophole in the system? Perhaps it's not worth doing. Chances are, if you personally benefit at the company's expense, it's probably best not to do it. Common sense really…

Accountability – Many things seem like a good idea until you are required to explain yourself. Honestly, I can't stop you from doing whatever you want at the time. However, running your proposed way of working by a colleague might highlight the reason for the current process. Just remember there will always be a moment when you have to give your reasoning to somebody else. You never know, there may be unintended consequences to your actions…

PSI – Chances are, if you are being pressured by other people into doing it, it's not a good idea.

Feel free to try new ways of working and find what suits you. It might take a while to find your groove, but the act of doing so is what apprenticeships are all about, learning. Remember, to some degree, you are limited by the rules of the organisation.

Just like Dick Fosbury, you have your own bar to clear. How you choose to do it is up to you.

Tip 7 – Gifts

Most of us are born with two gifts. The ability to listen and the ability to speak. I really don't want to teach you how to suck eggs. However, I have been a culprit, victim, and witness to the following on many occasions, so I think I can justify the next entry. Therefore, I mean the following in the nicest possible way; learn to keep your mouth shut and actively listen to what the other person is saying. I am constantly working on it myself, so by no means think of me as a perfect partner to conversate with. I sometimes zone out, cut people off or think more about what I want to say than the content of the other person's speech, even though I try to practice what I preach.

Spot the difference

I hope you noticed the word 'actively' in the first paragraph. If you didn't, then I'm assuming you're not 'actively' reading either. The addition of the word to the sentence is significant. There are two ways you can listen, and to explain, I will use music to highlight the differences. When completing a mundane task, it is common for people to play music to make these activities more tolerable. For example, when working or cleaning your house. However, the song is background noise. You know it is there, but it is not your primary focus. You can get a rough idea of whether it is an uplifting or mournful song by the melody, but not much more. Your brain is more occupied with what you are focusing on and less with the audio stimulation. That is 'listening'. Being aware of the presence of sound but not the content.

Actively listening occurs when your favourite artist releases a new album. You make a conscious effort to listen to the instrumental, the descriptive story being painted, any hidden messages, play on words, metaphors, similes, cadence etc. During such times, your mind is focused solely on the music. You are trying to gain as much information as possible from the audio and nothing else.

To be completely honest, I'm not entirely sure the following was required as it seems obvious. When engaging in verbal communication with others, it is vital you actively listen. If you don't, you will miss all sorts of information, and who knows what the outcome will be. At the time, you might be lucky and get away with it. However, after 2.5 years of experience as an apprentice, I am willing to bet it will come back and bite you on the arse at some point in the future. Believe me, you will have wished you actively listened. I bloody did.

Why Keep Your Mouth Shut?

From what I can recall about my time in school, a teacher's most common saying usually related to something about me either turning around or to stop talking. Both points were for good reason. If you're talking while somebody else is, you are not actively listening. You're probably not even listening at all. Not only are your actions disrespectful to those speaking (apologies to all I have done it to), but it also leads to three subsequent consequences.

Frustration – I've lost count of the number of times I have been part of a conversation where an unnecessary professional debate, to put it mildly, has ensued. It usually manifests from somebody not actively listening. They are more concerned about saying whatever thought has just popped into their mind, regardless of recently articulated comments. People debate topics that do not need to be, tempers flare, and body language and tones change. When you finish reading, you should google 'Wise Old Own Poem'. It explains my point in 34 words.

Time – I think I speak for most people when I say the shorter a meeting, the better. In fact, I will go one further. The fewer meetings, the better. If it's scheduled to be 30 minutes, I don't want to still be sitting there 45 minutes later unless it is for a necessary reason. Time is intertwined with frustration because, by not actively listening, you end up wasting so much time. Questions are asked when the answer was already provided, unnecessary debates, irrelevant anecdotes, repetition of information, and so on. Chances are, as an apprentice, you will be busy and have places to be and things to do, so time is of the essence.

Learning – I get it. Things are boring but more about boredom later. You cannot learn if you don't actively listen. You will not acquire any new knowledge. You might be able to get away with it for a short while, but after a month or two, you are now standing at the bottom of a steep mountain, so enjoy the climb.

Here is another thing to consider when you are an apprentice; you are now part of a business network. You will build connections on a daily basis with those from your team, different departments, or external people such as suppliers and customers. Somebody from somewhere can approach, email, or call you at any time, asking for information. You may not know the answer as it is above your pay grade, in which case you can explain. However, if they know you should be aware of such information, it is very tricky to get yourself out of the conversation whilst saving face. Sometimes your support won't be there. My manager once went on shared parental leave for a month, and I had to keep the department afloat. Not having a safety net really opened my eyes, as well as everybody else's, to how little I actually knew.

Making actively listening easier

It is a difficult skill to teach yourself for a variety of reasons. It requires mental discipline, especially if you are participating in long meetings or calls. Another factor to consider is that you may have to break some of your habits, which is tough. Unsurprisingly, I have noted a few things that can make active listening easier.

Use paper and pen – Or some sort of note-taking device. I think it is fair to assume most people cannot remember everything. By having the ability to take notes, you can make however many reminders you need to. Knowing you do not have to rely on the old grey matter is an enormous stress reliever. Remember earlier I mentioned people say whatever comes into their mind? Well, with the ability to take notes, you can write down your comments, analyse them and then share them when the time is right. The same goes for clarifying details. Jot these down to create a memory jogger rather than trying to remember an ever-growing list.

Shorthand code – The first time I took minutes, I was bloody awful. In my defence, I had never done it before. I tried to write everything down verbatim. From the start, I was doomed to fail. I realised I needed to develop a code to get all the information down whilst people were talking. Unfortunately, my advice ends here because it is specific to your apprenticeship. You have to create something personal based on your working environment and personal preferences. I suppose a universal rule I would propose is KISS.

If unsure, ask – You are learning, after all. The number of people who will help explain things is surprising if you politely explain your predicament. In the workplace, silence implies you understand, so speak up. Acronyms, technical terms, people's roles etc are also handy things to understand, as people will often reference them on the assumption everybody knows what they mean. If you don't, then you are essentially just listening. You acknowledge words are being said but are also unaware of their meaning.

Obligation – Don't feel required to talk just because you are present. If you have nothing to say, then there is no need to speak. Take thc time to process what you hear and only pipe up when you feel it is required.

The gift of listening outweighs the gift of the gab.

Tip 8 – Ignorance

Let me address something straight away. I'm not calling you ignorant. Rather than just insulting you, Tip 8 is more about trying to avoid situations in which you don't accept your own ignorance. It sounds peculiar, and it could have been just me being me, but I came to realise there are various reasons why it occurs.

Embarrassment – Who wants to admit, especially to a group, they do not understand the discussion taking place? I presume very few. While some people seem to think they know everything, such individuals are well beyond help. Let's be honest. They would have claimed to have known about all of these chapters beforehand anyway. Nevertheless, assuming you aren't the know-it-all type, here are two things you should consider:

1) You are entitled to ask. If you want to go to extremes, you do have freedom of speech.
2) Nobody really minds you asking, and you're overthinking it. You're an apprentice and there to learn. One way is through asking questions (to get more of those puzzle pieces). Chances are you have built up the situation in your head about what others

will think. Everybody in the discussion will probably forget what you asked by the time the conversation is over anyway. Who knows, maybe it is a bloody good question, and maybe nobody else had thought of it, even a simple one!

Timing – There is a time when it is acceptable not to know something and another when the lack of knowledge is unacceptable. At some point, there is a cross-over where you transition from one to the other. As a slightly over-the-top example, it is acceptable not to completely know the alphabet when you are two or three years old. It is unacceptable when you are 18 (except for those with learning difficulties). It is worth considering before you ask your question. However, it does not prohibit you from continuing, should you wish to. Long story short: Should you know the answer by now? Conveniently, that question flows into the next piece of advice.

Think – Is it something you should really be aware of by now? Do you have the answer and are just not thinking? Why don't you know? Have I come across the information before? Can I quickly find the information myself by searching documents, emails, chat messages etc? The reasons I listed these questions are twofold.

1) It is a little embarrassing when you ask a question, get the answer, and think to yourself, "Oh yeah, I did know the answer." Chances are, it was about something you really should have known about. Maybe you had other things on your mind, a lapse in concentration or your memory had genuinely failed

you. However, if you really put the effort in, it is remarkable what you can recall.

2) It gives you confidence. By thinking hard, you have covered all bases using the questions above. Therefore, it is only right you begin warming up your vocal cords.

Repetition – I'm not sure if the following is an experience anybody has had, but I'm writing it anyway. At one point, I found myself doing the same things repeatedly, day in and day out. There are pros and cons, but without blowing my own trumpet, I became bloody good at them. However, one outcome was I began to think I knew everything. It's a bizarre occurrence and, on the face of it, seems ridiculous. I guess it was a trap I fell into because the constant repetition made me think I knew all about the apprenticeship. It created a chain reaction. Repetition led to boredom, resulting in losing motivation, which made me deaf to others or unwilling to learn. Therefore, nothing new happened, reinforcing a belief that I knew everything, and the cycle continued.

Snowball – It's fascinating how many things link together, as mentioned in Tip 4. If you pay close enough attention, you can see how seemingly unrelated matters affect one another. It is also frightening how quickly things can get out of hand or run away from you. You may already have seen it in action because you probably have experienced the feeling growing up. You don't pay attention in one lesson, no problem. The workload to get back on track is manageable. After 10 lessons, you are significantly further behind in a relatively short period of time. Your coursework piles up. The trouble is, you have coursework from other subjects to work on too. Now, which do you focus on? You stay up late or rush to complete the work. You don't sleep well, become irritable, and your grades slip. Not paying attention during one has knock-on effects on others. As I'm sure you have figured out, the same applies at work.

Acquisition of knowledge

CBA – Is saying "CBA" still a thing? Well, if you ever wondered if I was out of touch, I think my question answers your question. Anyhow, in case the acronym has already gone out of fashion, CBA stands/stood for Can't Be Arsed or Can't be Asked. After researching, I'm still not sure which one it is. Pushing my linguistic intellect aside, yes, there will be times when you won't be bothered about trying to learn even though you know you should. Everybody has their days of minimal effort for a multitude of reasons. Should you get off your arse and study? Yes. Will you? No, or it is unlikely, at the very least. What you do in your lax mental state is up to you. I'm just making you aware of the consequences.

Acknowledge – I picked up a phrase from somebody on a call once. It was "apologies for my ignorance". They then proceeded to ask their question. There was something that surprised me more than anything. The speaker was a senior member of the company. The nature of the opening line sets the tone for the question. I wouldn't use it every time as it may lose its effect. However, it sure is a clever way of mitigating the associated embarrassment of the admission.

Pick and choose – Maybe the current situation is not a good time to ask your question. Instead, pick somebody out who you have a good relationship with and ask them afterwards. Therefore, you are not asking an audience, just a friend. Depending on their availability, it is also possible they will spend more time with you explaining than those in the meeting or call would have done. It might not be obvious, but there is a skill in picking the right time and person which comes with practice.

Ownership – Alternatively, you can teach yourself. Potentially the best choice for two reasons. First, you have complete autonomy over the way you learn. Second, it creates a brilliant gateway to speaking to others. Approaching an individual and explaining you have tried to educate yourself is far better than asking someone to put the spoon in your mouth without having tried to yourself. You can explain what you know, and they can correct or expand on your knowledge. From there the two of you can have a productive discussion.

Reputation – Furthermore, if you discover there is no available information, and you go away and learn about it yourself, then it is likely there will be others who also didn't know either. They might have been too shy/embarrassed to ask. By creating something that can be shared, you can help others and have a positive impact. Provided there is recognition of your work, you will boost your reputation and how you are perceived.

An individual who claims to know all is more ignorant than one who knows nothing but is willing to learn.

Tip 9 – Diet

Advancements in technology have helped develop our ability to stay fit or change our lifestyle through diet and exercise. For example, members of the public can now purchase smartwatches to count the number of steps or calories burnt. In addition, a wide range of machines and pieces of equipment are readily available depending on your personal requirements. If you have the money, you can work with nutritionists and personal trainers to maximise muscle growth, endurance, or strength. Alternatively, you can subscribe to various places and complete your own fitness classes at home. Depending on your fitness goals, you can buy powders to help slim down or put on size. Most fitness websites contain an array of supplements, vitamins and minerals that can be delivered straight to you. Some of these provide claims as to why they are better for the consumer than others on the market.

However, scientific studies can be easily skewed or misrepresented. There is debate whether certain online influencers surreptitiously take steroids to develop an Adonis-like physique in order to sell false promises via fitness plans to (what could be argued as) vulnerable members of the public. Men can become obsessed with the size of their arms, and girls (I imagine) feel pressured into how they look in certain clothes. We subscribe to companies who tell us what to eat despite having plenty of free online healthy eating advice. The simple rule being you have to be in a calorie deficit to lose weight. Only now are clothing brands finally shifting towards a more realistic model depicting the average man or woman. 'Big is beautiful' apparently empowers women of a particular figure even if doctors repeatedly tell them it is unhealthy. However, if you were to chant 'skinny is sexy', you would be berated for promoting anorexia or the stereotype that women should look a certain way. Some men feel they cannot pack on enough muscle even though they are already bigger than average. Love Island and the like create an unrealistic image to people of what men and women should look like and how we should act. Female clothing sizes make no sense because it is meaningless. Brands alter their sizing because, psychologically, women feel better purchasing a '10' rather than a '12', making them more likely to buy from a shop where they can fit into a smaller dress size. People become trapped in a cycle where they believe they can never lose enough body fat even though it is perfectly healthy and natural to have some (moderately speaking).

Considering the above, we still sit here today wondering why men and women develop self-esteem issues, lack confidence, or have some form of body dysmorphia. Depending on your perspective, technological advancement may have created more problems than it has solved.

In today's society, the idea of moderation and average have lost all meaning. There is something else which is okay in moderation, excuses.

You shouldn't ever make excuses!

I'm sure we have all heard variations of the saying. Whilst being a fair point, it is also not very realistic. You should also wake up early every day to make the most of your day, but it doesn't always happen. For me to tell you under no circumstances must you ever make an excuse is pointless because you will sometimes. What I can explain is the impact and how to can mitigate those feelings.

Organise – I used to make a lot of excuses. Conveniently for me, it was never my fault…

After thinking about the root cause, I discovered my rationale behind these bitches and moans was a lack of organisation. My working life was a mess. I had no structure, no lists, no priorities, I forgot what needed doing, and as a result, I was stressed every day. First, I had to explain (or get out of explaining) why I hadn't done the work without incriminating myself. Then, I'd get grilled sometimes, become upset (I'll say it with you equally as sarcastically, "Oh woe is me"), feel bad, and lack motivation to improve because I was always at a low point. As soon as I got organised, my frustrations went away. I created a 'to-do' list that I stuck to, formulated a colour scheme, prioritised, updated it daily and reflected so I could plan a productive day.

I don't care if it is pen and paper or electronic (I've seen people use everything from their phone to sticky notes), but having a to-do list alleviates many problems and therefore, fewer excuses are required.

Least worse – Great, you now have an organised list of things to do, but let's be real, you don't want to do the majority of them. Maybe it's due to your state of mind or because some tasks are legitimately dull and dreary. So how have you prioritised your task list? Perhaps by a deadline or alternatively by authority? However, to get the ball rolling, I recommend making a new list or filtering your current one based on tolerance. Which tasks do you feel most up to completing, and which would you rather forget about if you could? Completing tasks you can tolerate in your current mindset (usually described as 'quick/easy wins') shifts your mind into one of working, productivity, and, believe it or not, positivity.

There is a caveat: Be careful about incorporating the tolerance list method. If your line manager gave you an important piece of work and you didn't complete it in time because you were working through your 'quick wins', two words come to mind. Lead balloon.

Future – 'Don't put off until tomorrow what can be done today' – Benjamin Franklin (apparently). I would leave it there, but I have one more home truth on the matter. When you are in the mind frame of excuses, you create plans around the foundation of 'I will do it later'. Truthfully, the only intention here is to postpone your misery but guess what happens when the time comes? You create another plan because your misery has returned. Perhaps you just don't action your plan at all. Either way, the work doesn't remains incomplete. The future looks forever bleak, and the cycle continues. It becomes a rough place after a while. The longer you leave it, the more effort it takes to drag yourself out of the pit you created.

Stress – You probably already know about stress because of coursework. You put off the work for as long as possible whilst the deadline continues to get ever closer. You become more stressed, resulting in more procrastination as the mountain you face increases in size. You either rush to get it done, and the work is of poor quality. Others simply hope God's plan for you includes a get-out-of-jail-free card. Your longer terms stress will be immeasurable compared to the short-term misery of just knuckling down.

Relief – Being able to cross something off a list, especially a task you despise doing, can heighten your spirits. You no longer need to worry about any related emails, phone calls or conversations. At the end of the day, it is one less thing to do.

Try not to make too many excuses because there will be consequences, including potentially not passing your apprenticeship. If you continue to, before you know it, just like a diet, the scales won't be in your favour.

Tip 10 – Mud

For Tip 10, the chapter's name only really comes into effect at the end. I tried to come up with some clever link into carpentry based on the saying 'measure twice, cut once' and how you should 'think twice, send once', but it was terrible. Anyway, moving on.

Arguably, the most powerful tool we have at our disposal is language. Granted, that is not a new take, as it has been said for centuries. Language allows you to understand others and for people to understand you, enables you to get what you want, build relationships, solve problems, prove your innocence, and make others smile or laugh. Unfortunately, on the other hand, it can be used to create misery manipulate, deceive, hurt, and ultimately make things worse.

I think most readers will now start thinking about verbal interactions, but Tip 10 is more about emails and online messages. The question of why you need to think before you send can be split into two different categories.

Coherency

I don't think I'm the only one who spends far too long proofreading my emails. I get overly concerned with grammar, structure, formatting as well as the clarity of the message. It's not the worst trait to have, but eventually, I just have to send it, or the message will never appear in the recipient's inbox. Below are the things I noted over the years to help create the clearest email possible.

- Choose an appropriate method. Ironically, it might not be an email. Is it easier to call in response? Sometimes verbal communication is better than written or vice versa. After a phone call, a follow-up email detailing the points discussed is helpful, especially if your conversation/meeting was long, complex and/or important. In most cases, I prefer emails simply because it provides a trail of evidence, i.e. dates, financial figures, promises or attached documents that can all be used for future reference to support your claim. Plus, emails provide an opportunity for me to think before I 'speak'.
- Know exactly what information you need to send.
  - Think about it from the other person's perspective. No, it is unlikely they need to know a detailed minute-by-minute account of your weekend when they asked if you had a good one. What they will want to know the details of are the latest developments regarding the issue you spoke about last week. Granted, I provided an oversimplified example, but the principle applies to the context of messages.
  - Most people, I believe, hate long emails. There is an old comedic saying, 'Why use one word when two will do'. Ironically, I could have just written

'Keep it brief', but who doesn't love a bit of irony?

- Check for any basic punctuation and grammar mistakes. It makes a massive difference to what you say. In certain circumstances, it can change how the message is interpreted. Rather than me plagiarising other people's jokes, simply Google 'Why punctuation matters' and the point becomes rather apparent if it is not so already.
- Think about the format of your email. Have the content within sentences/paragraphs in a coherent sequence, for example, in the order of priority or date. You don't want the reader jumping around from one point to another.
- Use the simplest form to explain what is required (known as layman's terms). Don't overcomplicate things unnecessarily. You are doing nobody any favours. You will either get a phone call/email back asking for clarification, or the message will be misunderstood, and who knows what impact it may have.
- Avoid using all caps or highlighting words to bring specifics to people's attention. I quickly stopped when it was pointed out to me. It comes across as patronising. If you tell somebody about the 'below in red', they don't need the word 'red' in the colour red. Even if you intended to help those who are colourblind, it still wouldn't help when you think about it.
  - Those around you should be capable of reading and interpreting an email correctly. If they choose

to skim through and not pay close attention, more fool them. Why should you have to spoon-feed?

- Proofread and then proofread again. It's staggering how many mistakes you make in your first draft (as I'm sure whoever proofread *Apprentips* can testify)
- If you are unsure and think the email is significant, ask somebody to check it over for you. I did in the early days of apprenticeship number one because I thought every email was important. However, with practice, the need for support fades away as your confidence grows.
- If you have completed your proofreading and can't spot any more errors, try not to overthink. As I mentioned, I used to, but then I realised something. The majority of what I was worried about was just not going to happen. For most people, it is simply another email in their inbox. As long as the message is coherent and their questions have been addressed, people will reply (if required) and then file it away.

Impulse

I do not think it is as significant as being coherent, but it can still be a reason as to why you should think first.

- Not all emails are a source of misery. So just because you receive one from a particular individual doesn't mean you need to think 'Oh, what the fuck do you want now?' Although I'm sure many people do, me included.

- Be careful how you interpret the text. I usually start with 'Hi (enter name)' whereas some people begin only with the name, no greeting. Others don't even put your name. At first, I thought it was quite rude, almost like when telling a child off and you say just their name. I then realised that people respond differently and not to read too deeply. That is just one example, but it applies to other communication-based situations.
- It is very easy to type out a response in five seconds and hit send. I personally wouldn't. Mistakes tend to happen when you rush; such impulsive actions will only lead to further questions or confusion.
- Do your research before replying. Review your notes to ensure everything you are saying is accurate rather than an educated guess.
- Whether right or wrong, I recommend being polite and courteous. I've had to send many emails where I could have used every expletive under the sun, but the only person who would have lost out was me.
- Make sure you send your message to the right person and you call them by their correct name. Again, it happens when rushing, but I have had some awkward responses on a couple of occasions. In my defence, well, I don't really have a defence.

At the end of the day, how you communicate is up to you. I would advise to make sure your messages are as clear as day, not as clear as mud. I told you the title only came into effect at the end.

Tip 11 – Triangles

Relax, I'm not here to discuss Pythagoras' Theorem.

In my opinion, a peculiar phenomenon occurs in a professional working environment. It has perplexed me for a while because it makes no sense. I will try to reason out the possible factors for why it happens but also what you can do to overcome the enigma.

It starts when you are in your early years at school. The teacher sets you some homework and, in doing so, they cover three areas; what the work is, the reason behind it and the completion date (for future reference, I will refer to these three points as the 'Clarity Triangle'. Yeah, I'm not fond of the name either but I couldn't come up with a better one.) Now I understand juvenile schoolwork, relatively speaking, is simplistic. However, even homework such as "read and make notes on pages 35–48 of the textbook as we are going to discuss it next lesson" still follows the Clarity Triangle principle. Why? It is because teachers need to be sure you know exactly what you are required to do and the reason for it. Take any of the points away from the Clarity Triangle, and there is instant confusion and room for error.

As you enter the final stage(s) of your education, the work increases in complexity, e.g. essays or practical assignments.

The change in difficulty allows you to develop your independence in various forms. Hence, you no longer have to rely on your tutor to provide the answers. However, even for broad tasks, the Clarity Triangle still applies. For example, a teacher may say, “You must complete an X-word essay on (enter a specific question relating to the subject). The deadline is (enter date), and it makes up Y% of your final grade.” Of course, now it is incumbent on you to complete the task, but you still know exactly what is required.

Here is the perplexing moment. During both apprenticeships, I noticed the Clarity Triangle was no longer a foundation for communication. My mind was blown. I have been in many situations where I have been assigned work, and I was missing at least one corner of the triangle. At first, I did what was asked. Sometimes I didn’t because there was no deadline, and it was too late by the time I submitted the work. In other situations, what I produced was not aligned with the instructor’s vision. I eventually learnt it was best to ask questions to make sure I had all my ducks in a row before I began work. I might have annoyed people with my interrogation, but at least I was able to get it right the first time (more often than not).

Why does it happen?

Upon reflection, there are many reasons, and I don’t think blaming is the right course of action. These are just facts of the workplace. You might think I will criticise people for their poor communication skills, but no.

Poor communications skills – Okay, yes, there will be a handful of people who are terrible at articulating or transcribing their requirements. However, I feel like they are few and far between. Moving on.

Busy – Many people are, and therefore they may be hurrying around to get as much done as possible. When rushed off your feet, you don't always have the time to think clearly and methodically, as your mind is focused on other priorities. People aren't choosing to not provide useful information. It may have simply slipped their mind at the time.

Spoon feeding – Well, why should they? Sometimes you have to be proactive and use your brain. Although an obvious example, if somebody says a piece of work is "urgent", you shouldn't respond with "Okay, so when do you need it by?" because the answer is obvious.

Assumptions – It is common for people to assume you know the background information to the task they have assigned to you. Perhaps they thought you were at a specific place, meeting, or had been cc'd into emails. Therefore, they don't want to waste time by giving you the 'obvious' information they thought you already knew. The outcome is what you perceive to be vague instructions.

Interpretation – Just because you said something to somebody doesn't mean they will interpret your message as intended. You might think it was crystal clear, but others may think it was clear as mud. Ring any bells?

Sloping shoulders – A term used to describe an individual who deliberately delegates tasks to avoid taking accountability. The harsh reality regarding the working world is if somebody is unwilling to take ownership of an assignment, they do not care. Therefore, you will end up with the task (more on why in Tip 17). Likewise, if somebody is disinterested, they are unlikely to exert the required time and effort to guarantee the information being shared with you is clear, precise and detailed.

How to Overcome

Check before you reply – Twofold point here.

1. Re-read the original message or notes to check you haven't misinterpreted or misread the content. Pay attention to any keywords and consider what is said in the context of the situation. You might suddenly have a light bulb moment and be on the same page as the sender.
2. Re-read your reply. You don't want to come across as ambiguous. Check you have asked or answered everything necessary to prevent yourself from sending multiple clarifying responses. If your response involves documents, have everything attached or linked.
   - ➢ Side note: It may sound familiar but check you have the correct person's name at the beginning. Mistakes happen, but some are more embarrassing than others.

Ask – There is a bit more to asking than I mentioned at the beginning. Presuming you have read everything carefully, you may be left with a list of questions. The answers are essential as they are required before you can start the work. Consider offering a different choice of communication as it may be more efficient for both of you. Let's say you have a list of questions as long as your arm after reading an email. List them all down and then ask to speak on the phone, Teams or in person. Now you don't have to worry about formatting a rather complicated email. Sometimes verbal communication is more straightforward than writing as you get a quick and direct response, plus you can keep going back and forth until you are satisfied. A 10-minute conversation is way easier and faster than 10 long emails.

Yae or Nay? – You are now aware of what is required. Here is your dilemma. Do you say yes or no? It has been instilled in me through the advice of many people about the importance of 'perception and reputation'. Being perceived as valuable, helpful, and a team player all adds to your portfolio of soft skills. However, there is a catch. You can take too much on, and then the failure to complete the workload becomes detrimental to your image. If you promise you will do something, you had better deliver. A classic question you will come across is, "Do you have some spare time?" or "Are you able to help me?" As you should be eager and keen to build a positive reputation, it is far too easy to say yes without hesitation. You need to think carefully because your answer depends on many factors. The devil is hidden in the details. Get as much information as you can to understand the scope of the work. Then you can fall on either side of the fence.

If you say no, it is the end of the road. If you say yes, then you have two outcomes.

Set, aim, achieve – You know the details of the assignment, as well as the requested or negotiated deadline. You now have something to aim for. You work away ferociously, or maybe not in some cases. You complete the task in time and to a standard that upholds your reputation. Therefore, you have achieved your aim, a perfect outcome.

Set, aim, apologise – The opening lines are the same as before, except now you are working away ferociously only to find you won't uphold your end of the deal. Now you have to let the other person know, but there are elements to a well-crafted apology.

Apologies

Time – Here is where I think people occasionally fail, including me. As soon as you know, get in contact. If you conclude you won't complete the task two days before the deadline, don't wait until the person asks you where the hell it is to tell them. It just pisses people off, especially if they find out they could have had more of a warning. The reasoning behind their anger is that with more time comes more options to find a viable workaround.

Method – Depends on how urgent the matter at hand is. Face-to-face, phone, virtually (e.g. Teams) and email are all options, but you have to decide which is most appropriate. If it is urgent, then I recommend the order listed above. However, if the task is insignificant (and make sure it is), then you don't want to run around like a hot and sweaty headless chicken trying to find somebody when a simple email would suffice.

Reality – Obviously, you need to be sincere, but there is no need to grovel or beg for forgiveness.

Keep it brief – They don't need the whole saga or every minor detail (in most cases). Truthfully, it's likely they aren't bothered about those details either. They're only concerned with where their work is. ‘I got caught up’, ‘ran into unforeseen difficulties’, ‘it wasn’t processed in time’, or even ‘I forgot’ are succinct explanations. Should more details be beneficial to the recipient, then sure, explain.

Acknowledge – ‘Sorry for any issues caused’ or similar is a nice way to show you understand your actions have impacted others. Again, be rational. No need to kiss their feet.

Offer – Similar to when I mentioned going to your manager with a solution to your problem. After providing a brief explanation, offer a suggestion you think may help. For example, “I can send it over tomorrow”, “do you want me to speak to…”, and “I can show you what I have done so far…” are better than nothing. You now need to make sure you fulfil your promise! Fool me once…

Before you go

A few words of caution. An unspoken rule is you do not raise the fact somebody is sloping their shoulders. Even if you believe it to be accurate and others are aware, it is wise to keep your opinion to yourself and not let it be known in your responses. Leave it up to their manager to sort out. After all, you do not know what is going on inside and outside of work that may be affecting the behaviours of others.

Tip 12 – Public Speaking

It's fucking awful.

I'm joking. I promise you public speaking is nothing to worry about. Coming from a guy who chooses not to speak much and is not fond of becoming the centre of attention, it's quite a statement. Before I explain why, let me address the elephant in the room. I'm aware I already sound like every parent or teacher trying to reassure a nervous individual about an upcoming presentation. However, the following pages are based on my experiences. I've had my good ones, and on other occasions, I have bombed like a nuclear weapon. I've tried to avoid all the wishy-washy or dismissive comments. Everything I say is intended to put your mind at rest and give you confidence.

Spiders – Basically, Tip 5 again. Acknowledge you can't run away from it forever. At some point in your career, there is a high chance you will have to engage in some form of public speaking. It might not be imminently, but you will eventually. For example, your EPA (possibly). The reality might make you anxious but don't fight it now. Recognise it's a natural emotion and maybe even a phobia of yours.

Spiders 2 – There is nothing wrong with being scared of public speaking. A fundamental skill is controlling your psychological response so you can still think clearly about the situation. If you let it get the better of you, the ordeal becomes a self-perpetuating cycle. Eventually, you become so overwhelmed by public speaking you view it as an impossible feat. The following sections are designed to help you and even answer some of your questions.

Reality

Okay, before you even begin creating a presentation or writing a script, let's put things into perspective.

What are you doing? – You're only talking to a small group of people (most likely). You're not Freddie Mercury preparing to perform to a sold-out Wembley stadium. An even more simplistic view is that all you are doing is talking. Just talking.

Significance – Remember, you are an apprentice. The topic is unlikely to be of such importance where the organisation's future depends on it. Your presentation will likely be a high-level summary of a subject you are familiar with. Fear will lead you to believe your presentation is the most important event ever when, within the scale of your career, it is not even a drop in the ocean. Once finished, you will probably have forgotten about it in a week. Sure, way further down the line, when you are qualified and experienced, you may have some significant presentations to do. Still, it is improbable to be now.

What if you mess up? – Well, you mess up, but it's normal. Everybody does at some point. I highly doubt the stock market will crash and begin another recession. You might forget what you want to say or suffer a slip of the tongue, but ironically, you can talk your way out of these situations. I've heard people say, "Sorry, what I meant to say was", "Apologies, I've just had a bit of a mind blank", or they can make a joke out of the situation. The crazy thing is people just accept these moments. You have been honest. They know mistakes happen, and life goes on. As mentioned before, nobody is perfect.

People will judge me – Yeah, to some degree, just not as much as you think. In all honesty, many of the people listening won't remember most of what you said in a week or less. It also explains why you share your slides with those present afterwards. The audience is there to take note of the information they need, ask a question or two and leave. For them, your presentation is just one of many things they need to attend / complete during the day.

What-ifs – My favourite response to people who ask, "But what if (x) happens?" before proceeding to tell me an elaborative hypothetical situation is to say, "But what if it doesn't?" If you can control something, then focus on mitigating those possibilities. If you can't change certain factors, why worry? There is nothing you can do about it. We would never get anything done if we all thought of 'what if' scenarios and worried about them. Only be concerned with what you can control.

Preparation

The thought of making a presentation can be stressful. Here are a few tips I discovered or have been told that are worth sharing.

Creation – Personally, the most stress-free way to make a presentation is as follows.

- **Content**: Brain dump anything and everything which comes to mind. Words, phrases, pictures, numbers etc. It will be messy, unorganised, and incoherent, but you have made a foundation.
- **Order**: Start moving information into their relevant categories. Don't delete anything or read too deeply into what you have written. Just focus on grouping. Again, the document may still look messy once you're finished.
- **Cutting**: Keep asking yourself two questions. 1) What is actually relevant to the topic? 2) How much time do I have to speak? These two requirements will make the decision-making process regarding what to keep/delete easier. If unsure, make a note of the material somewhere else. You can always add the text again or mention it as part of your dialogue without the information being included in the presentation.
- **Details**: You can focus on sourcing those figures, charts, and names you couldn't quite remember earlier. You know precisely what you are looking for and where it sits within the structure of your presentation.
- **Aesthetics**: Once everything above is done, you can start exploring colour schemes, fonts, etc. I suggest keeping it simple. Don't go OTT with animations and sound effects. You're there to present some information, not make an Oscar-worthy production.

- **Make it your own** – I have stated the following point several times already, but you are an individual. You and I probably share things in common, but how we act may be different, presenting being one of them. Personally, I prefer not to have a script. Just pictures on the screen with a few words. Find whatever works for you, as you have to be comfortable with what you are working with. If you haven't developed a style, then experiment. You are (I'm guessing) young, so now is the time to test different ideas but believe in yourself. Don't feel pressured to present in a certain way only because others do.

It is possible you may have to present sometimes without utilising PowerPoint. For example, updating the team on a project or reporting on the information in an Excel spreadsheet or a PDF. Assuming you have the documents available, you can jump to the next section, practice.

Practice

Presentations will mess with your head because you won't be able to stop thinking about them. Lucky for you, you can use that to your advantage. Practising is vital but it doesn't mean going from start to finish every time. You can pick and choose what you rehearse. Plus, there are also plenty of opportunities to practice. You might want to rehearse your introduction when making a coffee, slide 6 while showering or even test yourself on the order of your presentation. Basically, just keep running through different parts of your presentation until it all becomes second nature.

Exposure – Like most things, the more you do it, the less daunting it becomes. The rule applies to both practising and presenting in general. You want to increase your exposure to presenting as much as possible during your apprenticeship, as it may be one element of your EPA. Therefore, when it really matters, you will feel more comfortable and less anxious.

Slow and steady – When you are nervous, you begin to speak quicker than normal, and maybe you don't notice. While practising, without the audience, you may be lured into a false sense of security. You may believe when the time comes for your live performance, you will articulate in the same manner as you do at home. A skill you should practice now is controlling the urge to speak quickly. Personally, I found deliberately speaking slower when practising helps. Consciously speaking slower will initially feel odd, but eventually, it becomes more natural.

Timing – "I have to speak for 10 minutes", "Well, how long is your presentation now?", "I don't know. I haven't timed myself." I don't need to finish the rest of the paragraph as the point, I hope, is obvious.

5 whys – To solve a problem, you must identify the underlying cause. If you don't, the issue, in one form or another, will continue to persist. You can apply the same principle to your emotions. I won't go into too much detail about the '5 whys', but it's a method for identifying the root cause of a problem. You state the problem and ask why. With every response, you ask 'why?' until you cannot produce a suitable or viable answer. The root cause can typically be identified within 5 cycles, hence the name. For example (> = why?): I'm anxious about the upcoming presentation > I don't know what I'm talking about > I haven't rehearsed > It's not finished > I keep putting it off. The last answer is the root cause of your anxiety. I'm not saying it will work every time or in all situations, but it's worth trying.

- I have encountered a fair few people who are worried about public speaking. The majority had one thing in common: they had yet to begin preparing. Therefore, their thoughts and negative emotions originated from procrastinating, not the presentation itself. You feel nervous about almost anything if you haven't prepared for it.

Carry yourself– Even if you rehearse and prepare, you still might not feel confident when standing in front of an audience, which is natural. One thing I have been told is to act as if you are self-assured. Speak confidently and let your body language show positivity by looking at audience members rather than at the floor. In doing so, a positive feedback loop is created. You act confidently, the audience is more likely to be engaged. They also display signs of acknowledgement (nods of the head, smiles, looking at you rather than at a phone, indicating they are paying attention), which tells you it's going well. You gain more confidence, the audience becomes more engaged and the cycle continues.

I'm not jumping into the deep end!

Fair comment, and not really much point if you can't swim either. The following is really for those who are terrified of public speaking and believe they will never do it. To gain confidence, I recommend breaking it down into manageable steps, so here is a suggestion.

Stage 1 – A 5-minute presentation only to your manager (or colleague or even a family member if need be) on a topic of your choosing, preferably one you feel passionate about. Some may need to repeat stage one multiple times. Once you feel relatively comfortable, move on to stage two.

Stage 2 – A 10-minute presentation on a topic of your choosing but in front of a few more people.

Stage 3 – A 10-minute presentation on a topic relating to work you are familiar with, for example, what you learnt during your course so far, to a similar number of team members.

Stage 4 – A 15-minute presentation to the team on a topic given to you by your manager.

Now, these are just suggestions, and you can tweak the stages however you need so the development plan works for you. The point is to start relatively small with each step getting slightly more challenging. You get to build your confidence and avoid a situation where your first presentation is to multiple people. You're unlikely to be transformed into the next Christopher Hitchens or Martin Luther King when it comes to public speaking. Still, you may be a little less daunted by the prospect.

Without a doubt, public speaking is a skill, and it requires a lot of practice. Of course, you also have to be willing to accept positive and negative feedback. With that being said, either one is a lesson which is designed to help you improve.

I am also fully aware I have produced a rod for my own back here. Should *Apprentips* result in me presenting to people about these topics, I think it's safe to say they will have some pretty high expectations.

Tip 13 – Salt

Salt is an abomination. I've never once added it to the food I have been served, and I don't use it when cooking (unless it is for other people). It is often overpowering and has nothing on the best spice, pepper. Worst of all, it ruins chips, which should be a criminal offence. I only included my feelings on those ghastly grains because I wanted you to know how much I detest salt. Just a smidgen of the sodium chloride crap is too much.

Speaking of a pinch of salt, let's discuss the interpretation of comments.

I suppose there are no real rules for communicating which is weird given what Tip 10 was about. However, those were tips, not rules, and yes, I created the loophole just to annoy the pedantic reader. At the end of the day, your message (both written and verbal) can mean different things to different people simply based on their interpretation. One person's sincerity is another person's ambivalence. Confidence can be seen as arrogance and offended as overdramatic.

Your point being?

Just because you perceive something in one way does not mean it was intended as such. Sometimes you need to take things with a pinch of salt and accept not everybody communicates in the same way you do.

Vocal – So by now, you will be aware I swear. Probably more than I fucking should. I don't really have a good explanation, but for me, words of such nature are just words. They don't pack much of a punch or have a deeper meaning. Thinking about it, I use them more as fillers, if anything. However, swearing is up there with blasphemy or apostasy to other people. Now, as considerate as I am, occasionally, an expletive will find its way into my speech. Before chastising me (or others), consider the tone, body language and context, which are all important when deciphering what somebody means. Interpretation doesn't just apply to expletives but speech in general. I simply used these as an example.

Text – You can't interpret a message if it is in text form unless there is some associated context. For example, let's say I sent you the word 'perfect'. On its own, the message is entirely meaningless. However, if it is in response to you agreeing to help me, then it can be interpreted as positive. If you just told me you crashed my car, you could interpret my response as sarcastic. People use the English language in their own way, and how you perceive what they mean is up to you. In all honesty, nine times out of ten, they are just words with no real undertone. (Statistic is not validated. Used as an expressive term to mean most of the time.)

Emotion and background – There is a near-endless list of reasons why people use the words they do. Everything from how they were raised and where to the type of day they are having, which has its own list of variables. However, these factors make people unique, and their words might not be intended to appear malicious. It's just them. Perhaps they saw the red mist, and you were at the wrong place at the wrong time. They may apologise afterwards, so you just have the take the verbal barrage on the chin.

Deep dive – With the first three points, I think they can be summarised by the umbrella term of 'reading too deep'. Is the person trying to deceive you? Irritate you? Was it a lie? Did they say 'was' instead of 'is'? Who were they speaking about? I wasn't made aware. Why not? Have I just uncovered their plan? No, probably not. It is more likely your mind is searching for whatever possibility you are thinking of because, deep down, you want it to be the case. I hate to break it to you, but the truth is, probably far more boring and mundane than you imagine it to be.

Two sides – Most places have a rumour mill working over time. It is best to hear both versions before concluding and attempting to decipher fact from fantasy. I think it is human nature to believe what you hear and jump to conclusions because it is the only information you have. However, in an apprenticeship, hearing the other side can give you a complete picture when there are multiple people with different personalities.

Offence – I will talk about being offended more in the next chapter hence the brief comment. I just wanted to make you aware it was on my radar.

P.S. Don't take me hating salt with a pinch of salt. I wholeheartedly meant it.

Tip 14 – Rhino Skin

Two things to note. First, the next chapter takes a more serious tone, so it won't be as jovial as the others. Second, if Tip 14 offends you, read it again.

There appears to be what I can only describe as a desire to be offended in society now, and I'm not too sure how it all started. Cancel culture is rife on social media, and every term appears to be offensive to somebody, whether historically or at present. People are scared to voice their true feelings, comedy isn't the same anymore, and some don't like to hear scientific evidence if the data does not support their views. I think one of my idols summed it up best.

> "If someone tells me that I've hurt their feelings, I say, 'I'm still waiting to hear what your point is.' I'm very depressed how in this country [USA] you can be told, 'That's offensive!' as if those two words constitute an argument or a comment. Not to me they don't. And I'm not running for anything, so I don't have to pretend to like people when I don't." – Christopher Hitchens

My intention is not to turn you into a stone-faced, cold-hearted, emotionless being void of feelings. More to point out how the whole concept of being offended seems pointless.

Definition

So, what is being offended? As far as I can see, it is the feeling of being hurt by your own interpretation due to the personal significance you place on the words uttered by others. Granted, the topic here is subjective, and what offends one may not offend another. You may have your own definition, but I think mine encapsulates the emotion.

Purpose

I cannot see a beneficial purpose to being offended. What do you gain? Okay, you can label yourself as a victim, which some relish far too much. I've thought about offence a lot over recent months, and I can only find one reason for the increase in what people deem to be 'offensive'. I concluded it is all about power.

Those righteous societal crusaders believe being offended grants them the right and the power to shut down the centre of cities, compel others to change their language or thought processes even if unconscious, file complaints, claim compensation, demand others to be dismissed or 'cancelled' and to resurrect your past mistakes no matter how old, which means they demand lifelong perfection regardless of the context or age.

The reason 'I'm offended' wields power is because it is subjective. How can you deem another individual's claim as nonsense or baseless? It's akin to if somebody said, "My meal doesn't taste nice", or "I think their artwork is atrocious". Categorically proving them wrong is impossible. If you can't prove their view is incorrect, then, in some way, it technically means they are correct. Demands are made (compensation, amendments, apologies, etc.), and the appropriate punishment for the 'defendant' is considered. The result sets the tone for future cases where offence is the central claim, and the cycle continues. Therefore, the verdicts and penalties are consequential. In the case of offence, it tells the public what is now acceptable and what is not.

Add into the mix the financial implications from lawsuits, celebrities wishing to uphold a positive social image, a brand's need to cater to their customers, and the possible threats of protests (or even violence to some degree), and it is no wonder being offended, or even the potential risk to offend, can have such an impact.

So, what does it all mean for you?

Math

I never did statistics at school because, based on my previous test results, statistically, it was unlikely I was going to pass Math A-Level. All things considered, let's attempt to think about it from a statistical standpoint. Say you meet 50 people throughout your apprenticeship. You're going to engage with 50 people from different backgrounds with differing personalities, idiosyncrasies, morals, and interests, to name a few factors. To summarise, 50 unique people. You will almost certainly disagree with everybody on at least one thing. You want to take offence? God, you will become a miserable, loathing, spiteful individual as you will be offended multiple times a day. It's no place you want to be, especially if you are there through your own choices. Eventually, you will find yourself holding countless grudges, and the only thing you seek is revenge. Why else would you bother being fixated on the supposedly 'offensive' comment?

Survival

Want a realistic chance of surviving in the professional working world? You got to be tough! Ain't no place for weak chumps. How you define 'weak' and 'tough' is subjective. You will fare better if you can roll with the punches because people say what they think, and you might not like it. Some beat around the bush until no leaves are left. Other people have no filter and tell it how it is. The latter is providing feedback with the best intention, and it's their style. Getting upset won't change their argument.

The Working World

A company should have a clear set of targets for the year. Each department should then align its aims to contribute towards achieving the overall company objectives. These can then be broken down into smaller objectives to provide you with a set of targets in relation to your role and responsibilities. As part of the process, work activities must be prioritised, budgets must be allocated, teams must be assembled, and many difficult decisions must be made. The key to a company's success is collaboration across all departments. However, everybody is competing for the same resources (time, space, facilities, materials, money etc.) to achieve their objectives and here lies a problem.

The problem stems from resources being finite. Not everybody gets what they want when they want it. Throw into the mix more factors, such as company politics, potential hidden agendas, and conflicting departmental priorities, and it is no wonder tempers flare on occasions. Before you know it, words have been said in the heat of the moment resulting from the build-up of events. It happens, and I've seen it first-hand.

Maybe the statement wasn't as bad as you thought, or maybe it was a Shakespearean shower of shit. My point here is words get thrown around a lot due to the nature of business, and it's astounding how easy they can upset you if you let it. To be honest, it might not even be work-related. Perhaps something was said at the coffee machine about a non-work-related matter, and they might not have even been angry at the time. It could have been a poor choice of words or a misjudged joke.

I recommend developing a thick skin for your own sanity, especially if you have long-term career goals. I used to take many things to heart. Are far as I know, I didn't show it, although others may beg to differ. I tried to remain cool, calm, and collected on the outsider. Inside, I was apoplectic and also miserable. Looking back, I had no reason to be, and I can't even remember what I got upset about, just that I was.

Whilst trying to think of valuable points to help you, I ran into a problem I continually refer to. Being 'offended' is subjective, and there is always context to a situation. As you can imagine, applying a rule of thumb is difficult.

I personally think the best way to handle the situation is to make a joke out of it if you are blessed with quick wit. If you can't, just shrug your shoulders and show indifference.

Perhaps you have to learn to poke fun at yourself. I couldn't when I first started, and I worked in a builder's merchant. I quickly learnt how to because it was the nature of where I worked. If you really struggle, go somewhere, take a breather for a minute or two and reflect. Was it intended to be rude? What was the context of the event? Does it matter? Are you going to remember what was said in a week's time? Are you the one placing significance on the meaning when it was completely baseless? Are you overthinking things?

Based on your answers, you can either shrug it off and continue your day or get offended. If you are upset, then tell the person you are. Simply for the fact, their reaction may make you realise you are being a bit OTT (a look of surprise, for example). It also provides them with an opportunity to explain why they didn't think their action or comment was offensive. The conversation may result in them apologising to you. If you're offended but say squat about how you feel, it will happen repeatedly. Nobody changes unless they have a reason to, so don't assume they knew.

Based on your answers, you can either shrug it off and carry on with your day or get offended. If you are going to get upset, then tell the person you are. Simply for the fact, their reaction may make you see you are being a bit OTT (a look of surprise, for example) or they will at least explain why they didn't think it was offensive or maybe apologise to you. If you're offended but say squat about how you feel, it will just happen over and over again. Nobody changes unless they have a reason to, so don't assume they knew.

All of the above depends on who you are and your instinctive reactions to things. From my own experience, ignoring is better than taking offence. It is far better in the long run to have the skin of a rhino than to become a bull in a China shop.

Unfortunately, there may be a time when something happens. Something that is not a joke or a slightly sarcastic remark. There is no easy way to slowly break into the next chapter. It will be a headfirst dive into the deepest end of the pool.

Tip 15 – Harassment

You will notice there isn't a light-hearted, thought-provoking title. It is because, in any environment, harassment is a serious issue. I wanted the message to be direct, clear, and meaningful. Furthermore, the following advice isn't applied just to apprenticeships. Finally, I speculate Tip 15 will be longer than the others.

I debated with myself for a long time whether I should include the following content because I knew it would invoke a wide range of emotions. Furthermore, I do not think my stance is particularly popular from what I saw on social media when I was on it. However, to solve a problem, you need to have open and honest conversations, which can be difficult and emotional. So, before you form an opinion, please read it in its entirety. Consider I wrote it with the intention to help people and generate a discussion for the benefit of all.

Background

After a week-long search, on 10th March 2021, a young woman's body was discovered. It was Sarah Everard. She had been murdered while walking home. I'm not going to say the name of the man who murdered Sarah because I think it is far more important to remember the name of the victim rather than the murderer. The tragedy sparked a movement regarding women's safety, with women sharing their stories of harassment both in and out of the workplace. Posts were shared on social media about what people could do to help solve the incredibly complex problem of harassment and women's safety. For the record, I only chose to reference Sarah Everard because it was on the news at the time of writing.

I was not particularly vocal. I decided to stay quiet, not share anything or respond to those who had uploaded various posts. I still had a view, but I was considering the situation at hand. I understood the intention behind the drive on social media and what people hoped to achieve through such a movement. However, I did not believe the proposed solutions addressed the crux of the problem.

My Thoughts

There is a growing movement where people believe we can achieve a utopian society. A world where everything is perfect. There are no problems, no conflicts, and no inequality. All thoughts, feelings, needs and wants are considered and addressed. Everybody interacts amicably with everybody, without disagreement.

Not everybody believes in the notion, but enough people are pushing it for it to have created noticeable changes within society.

Why? – I don't think these particular groups understand or appreciate the level of suffering that has occurred throughout human history. You can read countless books and find endless hours of material online explaining how difficult life has been. Many of us have not been exposed to the possible catastrophes or atrocities others have lived through. Life, in general, has been stable and, dare I say, 'easy'. It is why I think history is such an important lesson at school. If you can understand the past, it helps you understand the present and even predict the future.

To be clear, I know not everybody of recent generations is living a life of luxury. Some people in the UK (and the rest of the world) still live in poverty and contend with difficult or horrendous circumstances, which many of us never even have to consider.

Who? – Here is what I find interesting. It seems to be those not struggling who push such the 'utopian' narrative. Celebrities complaining about how their already high-paying jobs reflect income inequality when there are individuals who are thankful just to receive a small pay packet. Students in universities complaining about the names of buildings and the history of its founder but are happy to still go and receive their degrees. Activists marching into restaurants, trying to stop people from eating while chanting 'meat is murder' when there are people who haven't eaten in days or have to sacrifice their own meal so they can feed their children. Most recently, people feeling entitled to shut down motorways and disrupt the lives of others due to their own environmental concerns.

What's the crux of the problem?

Schools do not educate young boys and girls about the real world.

At first, I thought there was very little I could do other than make sure I didn't do anything myself and keep an eye out for others. Then I had a realisation I was creating a platform of some sort. I am writing *Apprentips* with the purpose of helping, essentially, adolescents. Many of them are yet to experience many life lessons, so why should I exclude such a topic just because it may be seen as controversial when it is a real problem. I really shouldn't have to, but I don't see anything changing anytime soon, and younger people need to be made aware.

Accept

It applies to life in general, and I did write how I would be 100 per cent honest. I don't know your outlook on life and how you perceive people, but I believe the truth is as follows. There are some truly wonderful people who would give you the shirt off their backs. Treasure those people because they are few and far between but don't abuse their kind nature. The majority are in the middle. They are not as helpful as those mentioned earlier, but they are also not terrible people by any stretch of the imagination. I guess you could describe them as 'average'. A mixture of helpful and a pain in the arse at times. Then you have those towards the other end of the spectrum who appear to make your life as difficult and miserable as possible. Whether they intend to or not is another question. It could come down to a clash of personalities or maybe they are just a dick to everybody. However, one set of people makes these looks like angels. These are those who commit atrocious and heinous crimes. I don't need to state what type of crimes as you already know which ones I am referring to. The problem is you don't know where people fall on the spectrum. Choosing to view everybody positively, assume they mean well, believe they don't have a bad bone in their body, or even that they can and will change is a risky life strategy. The last person you met may have been a delight, but there is nothing to say the same applies to the next one. Perhaps through careful judgement mixed with a sprinkle of luck, I am thankful not to have encountered any truly despicable individuals. However, I know people who have, and the mind cannot comprehend how such a person can act in such a manner.

Red flags

There was an online movement called 'Educate your sons'. To summarise, the idea suggested that young boys should learn the correct way to treat girls/women as well as hold boys/men to account for their actions. As a result, males would change their attitude and be less likely to develop or act on their (supposedly) impulsive, violent behavioural traits. I could see the rationale behind it. I didn't think it would solve the problem as the solutions proposed were too vague to directly address the root cause. However, I could see the people's train of thought. I think the narrative needs to be (for both women and men) 'educate yourself' because we will never remove these horrific aspects from our society. Manipulative, evil, narcissistic, wicked and twisted people will always be around because human psychology is unbelievably complex. Why people turn out as they do can be due to numerous variables. In some cases, we have no idea how to solve them, even though we are currently trying.

I think we need to teach people why they need to be able to identify and spot the warning signs. So-called 'red flags' are actions or traits you experience that indicate potential future danger. Unfortunately, manipulative or controlling people are bloody clever, so are unlikely to show their true intentions for as long as is required. They can be the sweetest people at first, treating you as you always dreamt. They begin with small, inconspicuous actions/statements that escalate over time. By the time you realise, it is too late. Removing yourself from the situation becomes tricky, and you feel trapped. You have become tangled in their web. In some scenarios, the only way out is through life-changing, difficult decisions. Rather than relying on others not to be terrible human beings, you need to learn how to spot them and to stay as far away as possible.

I am not saying or implying the victim is at fault if they find themselves in such situations. It is far more complicated than I am making out. Nobody would be taken advantage of if it was so easy to avoid. I'm only saying I think a better approach to overall safety is to educate yourself rather than relying on others to have educated themselves and change their behaviours.

Safety

"Why should we have to?" was often asked during the movement. The question relates to the extra measures women were, and are, having to take to get home from nights out, walks from work, late-night runs etc. to maximise their safety. While, again, I can understand the rationale behind the question, I think there is an answer that, also, will not be popular.

Crimes of the most heinous nature are crimes of opportunity. The person is driven by self-centred motives, and they know what they are doing is going to (or at least should) result in some form of punishment. Therefore, they always try to be one step ahead of everybody else. The measures we have in place and ask people to follow are to mitigate the number of opportunities the culprit will have. Given the sad fact that opportunists will always be present in our society, they are recommended for a reason. I agree with you completely. Sarah did everything by the book as required, but as I said, people with such intentions will always find a way to be one step ahead and wait for the right time.

It's analogous to saying we don't need airbags, seatbelts, automatic emergency braking systems, and safety testing for cars because we should all be able to trust everybody on the road. We should educate drivers, and they should change their behaviours. But we have measures in place already. We do it via speed awareness courses, fines, driving bans, court-ordered retaking of driving tests and prison sentences. Despite everything in place, people still speed, use their phones while behind the wheel, drive while intoxicated, and race erratically down country lanes. We have the safety measures in place because we don't know who else is on the road and how they behave. As far as I know, nobody knows how to completely irradicate the problem in both cases.

I hope you never have to use the following, but it is still worth sharing. The next part is easier said than done. Don't think I'm ignoring complicated factors such as shock, injury, fear, anxiety etc.

So, what should you do if there is an event you deem to be harassment of some description? Again, the below is not just related to apprenticeships.

Do not stand for it

As awkward or tough as it may be at the time, you have to say something. We aren't talking about a barista who has made your coffee incorrectly. We are discussing your own feelings, privacy and/or personal space and safety. You must make your feelings known. It takes strength of character, but if you stay silent, it will only continue. Careful of the power of charm and charisma. I've heard of some cases where people let things fall by the wayside because of these two characteristics. It may sound trivial, but they are more powerful than you think.

Make a record

Write everything and anything down and/or take pictures. Grab paper, cardboard, napkin, phone, your hand, or whatever you can get your mitts on as soon as the event has happened. If the surface you have written on is not ideal (for example, a napkin), then as soon as you can, transfer your notes onto paper or a Word document and save both copies somewhere safe. The napkin as evidence, the transferred version for clarity and coherence. Write down every detail you can remember such as:

Name of person/people involved, any description of the person/people, date(s), time(s), any witnesses, statements made, locations, what happened in as much detail as possible, save emails or texts, take screenshots, how it made you feel and previous attempts to stop the harassment. I may have missed out on some factors you might want to include, but my point is what I made at the beginning. Write down everything and anything. Never think a detail is insignificant. Do it as soon as you can, too. It all matters.

Why? – What you are doing is collecting evidence and building a case for yourself. When it comes to the time you report the event(s) to the relevant authorities, you have evidence which supports your accusation. I choose the word 'accusation' because, at the time, legally, it is. Only after the evidence has been gathered and reviewed, suspect(s) had a chance to explain their side of the story, and a verdict has been issued can the term 'accusation' be replaced with the applicable adjective/noun (offender, guilty etc). I am not implying I or others do not believe the claim. It is because our legal system works on the basis of innocent until proven guilty' From a legal standpoint, it is an accusation when first discussed. It can take a long time to go through the investigation process. It may be mentally demanding on yourself as you might be asked to recall events. It's all for the greater good, so stay strong and keep moving forward.

Tell somebody

Speak to a parent, trusted friend, colleague, human resources, helpline or even a stranger if need be. If you are out somewhere, speak to the waiter/waitress, staff, manager, checkout person or whoever is around. Some places, like bars, have special code words you can say to alert staff about the fact you do not feel safe in the current environment. It takes strength of character, and you may feel uncomfortable, but for your health, safety, and well-being, you need to raise the alarm as soon as possible.

Dismissive – If you do tell somebody and you get a response along the lines of "Nah, they would never do such a thing", "You must have misunderstood", or "Oh, that is just (name) being (name)", find somebody else to speak to. You know what happened, and you know who was responsible.

Escalate – Getting nowhere? Move your claim higher up the hierarchy. I can't say the exact steps, but your company will have a grievance policy. Give it a read to work out what to do next. I'd love to say more, but every company is different, and I may hinder rather than help. Remember, you have a bank of evidence. If need be, outside of work, go to the police with the evidence you have.

Leave – Still getting nowhere and nobody listening to you? Leave. Okay, far easier said than done because there are multiple considerations. Still, in the long run, it is the best option. First, it gets you out of the environment. You no longer need to see the offender, which I imagine is traumatic, especially if on a daily occurrence. You may have to start again and be in a worse position from a career perspective, but it will only be short-term. Unfortunately, if you do not leave, things are more likely to worsen.

You are not alone

The onset of depression is no joke. Hopefully, you will have people around you to provide emotional and/or physical support, but if you don't, seek help through other means. I made a 'Useful contacts' section to save you from going online and doing the research yourself, although it does not include all available services. The contact information is only for national organisations, but you may be able to find help locally to you. These organisations exist for a reason, so somebody is always there to help you, even if not within your immediate sphere.

Life is unfair

Not to say your efforts are futile. However, in some instances, people do not get what they deserve. Proving somebody's guilt can be more difficult than it sounds for various reasons, so some people get away scot-free or with a lesser punishment. I imagine hearing such news can be soul-destroying, but the saying 'Life isn't fair' has been around for donkey's years and for a good reason.

Look out

Perhaps something isn't happening to you but somebody else. It's worth watching and looking for changes in people's personalities or behaviours. Not to say they have suffered harassment or abuse; it could be something completely different. Just asking a question or two may help the individual.

Probability

Like I said near the start, I hope you never have to use such information apart from the 'red flags' part, which is worth considering when you next take a break. I recommend applying the advice sooner rather than later. Unfortunately, I have no idea whether you will experience such people or events, but knowledge is never wasted. I mentioned probability just in case you thought I was implying it is a common occurrence in the workplace/life. However, it was not the image I was trying to portray.

Useful contacts

As mentioned, I thought it may be helpful to show where you can go should you happen to experience an event. Just remember, you aren't alone. People are far more open to talking about personal matters and more supportive than you think. Also, you were not to blame. I know words seldom help victims of such occurrences. Still, it is heart-breaking to read stories (or know of someone) who takes their own life because they felt like they had nowhere to turn. I have hesitantly opened up to some people about certain circumstances, and the response I received was surprising: compassion, empathy, the offer of assistance and a genuine listening ear.

Whilst the below is just a handful of options, you can find many more organisations covering a wider range of 'problems' (their term, not mine) at www.supportline.org.uk.

ACAS (Free impartial advice on workplace rights, rules, and best practice for both employers and employees)	www.acas.org.uk 0300 123 1100 Available Monday – Friday 08:00-18:00
ChildLine	www.chlidline.org.uk 0800 1111 Available 24/7
CALM	www.thecalmzone.net 0800 58 58 58 Available 17:00 – 24:00 365 days
The Mix (Under 25)	www.themix.org.uk 0808 808 4994 Text THEMIX to 85258
National Suicide Prevention Helpline UK (18+)	www.spuk.org.uk 0800 689 5652 Available 18:00 – 3:00
Samaritans	www.samaritans.org 116 123 Available 24/7 365 days
Switchboard (LGBT+)	www.switchboard.lgbt 0800 0119 100 Available 10:00 – 22:00
Shout	www.giveusashout.org Text SHOUT to 85258 Available 24/7
Victim Support	www.victimsupport.org.uk 08 08 16 89 111 Online live chat Available 24/7

Last point

Previously, I discussed the difficulty of interpreting text. If, after reading, you still think my choice of words implies I am negating the issue, making light of, or assigning blame to victims, please understand your interpretation is far from the intended purpose. Granted, some things are oversimplified, but I tried to write as much as possible while keeping within the book's format and purpose. Nothing here was written with a sarcastic undertone. Nothing was intended to come across as flippant or dismissive. Tip 15 is an important message designed for an important topic.

Harassment, abuse, and assault are no joke in and out of the workplace. Please do everything you can to keep yourself safe. It may seem unfair you have to take such actions, but unfortunately, life is not fair.

Tip 16 – Balance

On paper, an apprenticeship is flawless. A company hires an individual who is there to learn by working for a small salary. By the end, they are qualified, knowledgeable, experienced, integrated into the team and can be taken on full-time. Therefore, the overall cost of the apprenticeship is an investment rather than an expense. On the other hand, if the individual is not up to standard, they can be dismissed much easier than a full-time employee, and the money lost through the investment is insignificant. It's a win-win. However, issues arise once you add real-life factors such as personal motives and business needs, which, funny story, nobody really talks about.

The underlying problem is a manager's job and reputation are scrutinised monthly, if not weekly. Their income is based on the success of their area(s) of responsibility, which is indicative of their performance. There is potential commission, bonuses, promotions, recognition and awards, future work, and retention of clients on the line in addition to a better lifestyle (higher salary, company car etc.) Furthermore, they are also responsible for other employees in many ways, including motivation and continuous development. Meanwhile, you, the apprentice, have your own list of concerns, mainly passing your course, completing any coursework, and learning as much as possible. But what if your list of priorities and the manager's list of priorities are fundamentally different? I think you can see where the point is heading.

It is a big problem for apprentices because what do you prioritise? The need of the manager and company or the needs of yourself? Tricky question because, in most cases, one loses out.

Unfortunately, it's worse on your side because you have minimal influence and authority. Trust me, I've engaged in numerous battles and seldom won. You have little negotiating power, and the manager has the final say. You can go above their head, but it's a risky approach. You risk damaging your relationship and reputation. Remember, you are an inexpensive resource in the grand scheme of the company overall. However, all is not lost.

Hymn sheet

How do you overcome the conundrum? To put it bluntly, sit down and have an honest discussion. Both of you have to be transparent in turns of what your priorities are. Your manager should have some background knowledge about what you need to do, but they might not know everything. Perhaps you need to explain your apprenticeship requirements in more detail or even correct their understanding. During the discussion, you may realise a percentage of your requirements do not align. The good news is that now all is out in the open. You can come to an agreement about these differences. You both must be willing to compromise, so don't think you can get everything your way. You can begin implementing the solution, which becomes a pattern, and eventually the norm. Sure, you can tweak and alter should circumstances change, but it means, from the start (or near as makes no difference), you are both singing from the same hymn sheet. I cannot really emphasise via text, but I place significance and importance on taking the recommended action. On my second apprenticeship, I engaged in conversation way too late, which was one reason why it turned into a disaster.

Solution over problem – Sometimes, not everything goes to plan, and life chucks an unexpected spanner in the works. It may mean you are back at square one, resulting in you now having an opposing agenda to your manager. Like before, you need to have an honest talk with them and go prepared with possible solution(s). The formula for the chat is, 'Here is the problem. Here is how it affects me and/or you. Here is what I propose. What do you think?' From the manager's perspective, speaking about a problem with no solution is not productive. Your proposed idea might not work for any number of reasons. However, it could either provide the building blocks for a different solution. At the very least, it shows you are proactive and not dependent on the manager to solve all your predicaments.

Workload

So, there is how to establish a long-term working pattern that (hopefully) suits both of you, all things considered. But what about the day-to-day balancing act of the work relating to the job versus the work relating to the apprenticeship course? Below is some advice, most of which are based on what I could do if I could go back in time and make my life easier (you may notice some sound familiar). I undertook two apprenticeships, and I royally fucked them both up with respect to coursework.

List – Write down everything you have to do. Even if it's a spontaneous thought about something way off in the future. Find one place to write down everything on your to-do list. It relieves the stress of remembering everything and is key to the next piece of advice (plus, it's satisfying to cross things off. Not the main point but still).

Prioritise – Similar to what I said in Tip 9. It requires skill to rank a multitude of activities based on their importance because how do you do it? By: Deadline? Delegator? Complexity? Duration? For a couple of tasks, it is relatively simple to work out, but once you start being assigned multiple tasks with multiple factors, it becomes tricky. You have to decide what works for you because your situation is most likely unique. However, I highly recommend reviewing your 'to-do list' regularly throughout the day just to check your order is still correct. Circumstances can change rapidly, which can push something up or down your list.

No – You can decline people's requests when they ask for assistance. While you want to display your willingness as a team player, it is important you know your limitations. Promising work you cannot complete will only create problems for yourself and others. If you are going to pile your plate your best, make sure you can eat it all. You can decline to help in various ways, but they usually follow the following principles.

Understand what the task is and when the deadline is. It would be foolish to answer before knowing what you are getting yourself into.

1) When declining, be polite in your response, although common courtesy should go without saying.
2) Explain why you can't. No need to go into minutiae, but you can use various phrases that allude to your current workload.
3) Similar to the 'solution over problem' paragraph. It is beneficial to suggest a compromise. For example, 'Unfortunately, I can't today, but I could work on it early next week?' You put the ball back in the other person's court while still showing you are still willing to help.
4) Don't lie. If you say you don't have capacity but then you are seen having several long breaks and minimal time at your workstation, you're just going to aggravate other people and develop a reputation.

People understand, so don't be afraid to say no, but only if you have a genuine reason. In my experience, other people will respect your answer, provided it is constructed using the above advice.

Extra hours

Occasionally, you will feel you have to work outside of your contracted hours or designated shift. I've done it so many times, and it sucks. My two takeaway points from those experiences are:

1) On most occasions, it was my fault due to poor time management.
2) It isn't always necessary. A manager of mine once told me, 'You always have tomorrow.' He was right. Think carefully about the next day before committing to your evening shift.

Coursework

Evidence – From the beginning, keep an eye out for what you could use as evidence in your apprenticeship. Make saving/uploading potential items a habit. When submitting, you are not stressing about trying to find something from months/years back. Efficient collecting of your KSBs is the key to a less stressful apprenticeship.

RLL (Reflective Learning Log) – Complete it every week without fail. If you don't, before you know it, you have 30 to fill out retrospectively, and it's near impossible to complete. Your tutor should provide feedback from a quality and content perspective, but anything is better than nothing.

Discipline

I went through a phase of being disciplined, then not and then back to trying to become disciplined. During the journey, I learnt two things.

1) The balancing act is easier when you're disciplined. You manage your time better, you're more productive, you don't worry about deadlines, 1:1 reviews are more straightforward because you completed the work you should have done over the

week. In addition, your manager will also have formed a higher opinion of you because you achieve what is required. I don't have an exact quantitative figure, but it feels 10x easier and far less stressful.

2) It's slightly terrifying how easy it is to spiral out of control. For me, it only took a few events in close succession and boom! I didn't so much spiral, more of a nosedive. You must pay close attention to your actions and identify when you begin to lack discipline. From my experience, very few people, if any, will be honest enough to tell you directly that you need to buck your ideas up. Nobody did with me, perhaps because I was hiding it all as best as I could. If I had my time again, I wish somebody had figuratively slapped me in the face and said, "Oi, pull yourself together," because, as harsh as it seems, it would have prevented many a problem which were my own creation. I'm not blaming others when I say that. I still fully acknowledge it was my fault and take responsibility.

I struggled to describe just how difficult it is to pull yourself back together. First, you have to want to change. Next, you have to understand how your behaviours are causing you the misery you are experiencing. It can be hard to admit because it puts the blame and responsibility on your shoulders. Finally, you have to break your bad habits. It is precisely what I am trying to do, and it requires a lot of effort, energy, willpower and sacrifice. The long-term benefits will be worth it, but I wish I had stuck to my original mentality.

Tip 17 – Bottom of the Pile

At the start, I said I would provide honest advice about apprenticeships. Unfortunately, although a point you may have already considered, Tip 17 is a real kick in the nuts.

An organisation is a hierarchy based on two factors, competency and experience. Your position in the company is not a direct correlation of the two attributes, but for the most part, those with high levels in both tend to be more towards the upper half of the hierarchy.

As an apprentice, it is almost guaranteed you will have very little of either. Therefore, you're placed at the bottom of the hierarchy. You won't be there forever, but you might as well know your place as well as the subsequent pros and cons. Nobody really discusses it, but you have the right to know.

While writing, I reflected on my thoughts about being at the bottom. I thought I should be working on the more fulfilling tasks. I pushed my apprentice title aside and tried to forget I was at the bottom. I began to believe I was higher up the hierarchy than I actually was and became frustrated. It's no surprise my mindset led to all of the negative aspects I listed previously. Perhaps the root cause was a sense of arrogance or self-entitlement. Regardless, I missed out on learning opportunities and had to spend a lot of time changing my mindset and dragging myself out of the pit I had created. Anyway, I've wiped away my tears, so moving on.

The Negatives

Pass the parcel – Except it is one nobody wants, and guess who has hold of it once the music stops. You. The parcel represents the tasks others are too senior to do or simply don't want to do. The reason you can be lumbered with a mundane set of tasks is because you're earning your stripes, and at the end of the day, somebody has to complete them. I've had everything from sweeping warehouse floors, writing labels, organising over 150 folders and coffee runs. It also corresponds with the fact you are inexperienced, so you cannot be assigned any large projects which require a certain level of knowledge and ability, although your time will come. By no means am I saying that every single thing you do during your apprenticeship will be tedious. In fact, far from it. I'm just making you aware of the reality. Not everything will be glamorous and exciting. Remember that no matter what task you are assigned, you should do it to a high standard and be treated with common decency. After all, working is a two-way street.

3 horsemen – Boredom, lack of motivation and procrastination make up the mental apocalypse. There will be various reasons why such emotions and actions arise, but the point is to be aware you will experience these. Truthfully, only you know how to stop yourself from becoming bored and procrastinating. I highly recommend nipping these in the bud as soon as possible because, rather quickly, you will develop bad habits and begin spiralling downwards. Coursework is affected, mistakes are made, and all the points I discussed previously come into play. You become miserable, unmotivated, challenging to work with, and possibly even cynical. It is a tricky place to get out of. I've been there, and it's no fun. I'm sure plenty of other people who worked with me can testify I was indeed such a person for a time.

Futile thinking – I've been pondering a question for quite a while now. Does everything have a purpose? The answer sounds obvious, but when you think about it carefully, you might realise you were wrong. Inevitably you will be assigned a task and think, 'What's the point?' which is a reasonable question. Now I don't know where you are/will be working or what you do/will do, so I'm unable to provide a direct answer. Instead, here are some home truths about seemingly, purposeless tasks:

- It is a monotonous task with a purpose, but you don't want to do it, so you convince yourself there isn't one.
- It's all part of a bigger picture. A company will only tell you so much information. You can keep asking questions, but you might not always get a satisfactory answer. It will all come to light eventually.
- The company is paying your salary and wants to get their money's worth. You sitting there doing nothing is wasteful, so a task is at least getting some value out of your financially inducing time.
- Your manager works in mysterious ways. It's just part of how they run things. Some people are enigmas.

The Positives

You're surrounded – The amount of free knowledge and wisdom you have from those more experienced than you is invaluable. Why not make the most of it while you have the chance? Knowledge is never wasted. Become a sponge and soak up everything you can. I didn't maximise such opportunities as much as I should have, but I wish I did because it would have made my life easier.

Build reputation – If you are assigned a task, and it seems very simple, long and/or boring, just know there is an element of smoke and mirrors. Your line manager isn't desperate to see if you can clean something or file a document. What they are concerned with is: What standard do you hold yourself to? Are you taking a lot of breaks? Are you easily distracted? Do you moan straight away? How do you operate when it appears nobody is looking? These are all categorised under your work ethic, and people can tell an awful lot about you just by assigning you a small piece of work. Do these well, and people will start using more positive than negative adjectives when describing you. Colleagues talk more than you think.

Could be worse – Yeah, it's possible. You got a bad job to do? Well, it's almost certain somebody else has something worse on their to-do list. I'm not saying you should be overly thankful for what you have to do. However, the task isn't the end of the world. As so many people have said to me before, 'We aren't saving lives,' which is a fair comment. The question I now have is, what is said to people who are actually saving lives? What phrase do they use to put things into perspective?

Temporary – Whether something is good or bad, eventually, it has to come to an end. You can apply such logic in two ways. First, look at the bigger picture. You know the end date for your course, so you only have X number of days left. Your suffering is not eternal. Now, look at the smaller picture, the task you are doing now. Hypothetically, let's imagine it is soul-crushingly boring to take to the nth degree. It will only last a limited amount of time. Maybe in 30 mins, you will be done. If a task is of a sizable duration, break it down into manageable pieces. Either way, it will be over, and you can reward yourself.

Grounds you – The final point requires some imagination, but I believe it is a consequence of being an apprentice. As mentioned, one day, you will have climbed the ranks, and somebody else embarking on their career will be fulfilling those duties you once dreaded. Who knows, you might even be the one delegating it to them. You should remember how you feel now so, in the future, you can treat those you take under your wing with respect and not end up holding hypocritical or unrealistic views. It doesn't take a genius to see the managers who remember their roots and those who don't.

So, there we have it, a few things to note which, in all likelihood, nobody will ever talk about at work. I'm not implying you should never moan about something or have a vent every now and then. Come on, you're only human. All I wanted to do was highlight the reality of what life is like at the bottom.

Tip 18 – Atheism

I don't believe in a God, or at the very least, I find the existence of one incredibly unlikely based on the evidence available. Within the realm of religion, I am far from an intellect who can provide a detailed exegesis of the various religious scriptures around which others centre their lives. As far as I'm concerned, those pushing religious agendas appear to have no reliable evidence and can only ask non-falsifiable questions to which they also do not have the answers, although they may claim otherwise. Somebody else I spent a lot of time not believing in was myself. Hell, I was even hesitant to get *Apprentips* published.

I think a lack of self-belief is a common mindset, especially among the youth of today.

Whilst the evidence for a divine being is virtually non-existent, so is the evidence for why you should not believe in yourself.

Evidence

There is nothing to suggest you cannot achieve something. People may tell you otherwise, but who knows what their motivations behind such comments are: spite, jealousy, doubt, lack of imagination and the list goes on.

Every industry has its pioneers, and people are constantly pushing the boundaries of what is possible. Not to say you are going to do the same, but maybe your goal(s) and dream(s) are your own equivalent but on a personal level. If you have your heart set on something, go and get it. There will be good and bad times like with all things, but as long as you keep believing in yourself, you can achieve anything. Eventually, more people will buy into your pursuit, and those who still haven't aren't worth keeping around. Cliché, I know, but nonetheless true.

Paths

There is no set path you can follow when it comes to your apprenticeship. Sure, the company will / should provide you with a plan in terms of key milestones etc., but the actual journey between each is non-existent. You have to forge your own path as you're walking it. Life works in mysterious ways (not because of God), and sometimes it is in your favour and other times not. How you deal with these alterations to your meander through your apprenticeship is up to you.

Social media

It started off great. My memory isn't the best, but I vaguely recall the days of Myspace and even Bebo. Upon reflection, it all seemed so innocent. Looking at the likes of Facebook, Twitter, and Instagram today, it appears to be a wash with fabricated, filtered, and fake posts designed to 'get likes' or show others their life is far better (or worse in some cases) than it really is. Fake news was, for a time, the answer for anything which didn't align with somebody's view and conspiracies can amass considerable backing because of the 'fake news' available online. Influencers seem to be massive at the moment, and many are all about making money (sometimes via scams) or achieving a dream body. As touched upon in Tip 9, there is conflicting information about how you achieve such a result. Some swear by products or services which they just so happen to be sponsored by. Some say wake up early and say you don't need sleep, whereas others say the opposite. Finally, whether you should invest in cryptocurrency depends on who you follow. It can be very easy to get caught up in a world of 'successful perfection' as I call it. Focus on yourself and go at your own pace, don't worry about how everybody else is doing all of the time.

Relative

Linking into the previous point, Max Verstappen and I were born within a few months of each other. We can argue the toss of who has a better lifestyle, but we all know it's him. He travels the world driving every petrolhead's dream, has sponsors left, right and centre, and earns millions of pounds a year. I also presume he rather enjoys it.

Me? Well, I have nothing along those lines. My Vauxhall Corsa is far from an F1 car, and the only time I get to travel to a new location is when I book a holiday. I don't have millions in the bank, and I can't say I currently have job satisfaction. Considering we are near enough the same age, I should be devastated, right? Why haven't I reached the same heights at the same time? I used to ask myself those questions when I compared myself to others (not just concerning Mr Verstappen, he was only used as an example). After a while,

I learned it wasn't beneficial or helpful, so I changed my mindset.

- As mentioned, everybody is following their own unique path. Why should you be so concerned about comparing when two separate lives are incomparable? We all have different upbringings (for example, Max's dad was an F1 driver), educations, strengths, weaknesses, friends, financial situations, interests, opportunities, blockers etc. You cannot compare your life to others fairly due to the potential number of variations.
- You have no idea what is real and what's not. The ways in which people can fake posts online seem to be endless. You could be getting down heartened over something that might not even be legitimate or real. Not to say, Verstappen faked his way to F1 glory by any means. More in the sense of social media, as I touched upon previously.
- Some people (like all those involved in F1) have worked bloody hard and achieved great things. They sacrificed a lot to get where they are and reaped the rewards for their efforts. Rather than being envious, see it as inspiration and take your hat off to them.
- Other people probably look and wish they were you. While I do not think Max wishes he could swap lives with me (I may be wrong, who knows), there are probably tens of thousands of others who look at mine / your position and would give every last penny they had just to be in your shoes, in some cases literally.

If you spend your life comparing yourself to others, you will only end up feeling low. There is always somebody better off than you in one way or another. Don't be too concerned about where everybody else is in their life.

Back to the point, you may not be a deity, but it does not mean you cannot believe in yourself.

Tip 19 – Quick Fire

These are the terms I wanted to make you aware of, but I couldn't waffle on for long enough. I still think they are of value, so rapid-fire explanations it is. These are all high-level summaries with plenty of further detail available online.

Basic salary – What the company has agreed to pay you before tax. It will most likely be x amount a year. The basic salary does not include things such as expenses, benefits, commission etc.

Payslip – Proof you have been paid the dosh you worked your fingers to the bone for. It will show the necessary deductions, such as taxes. I recommend checking your payslip because there can be errors. Most likely, it will be electronic, although I'm sure there are companies still using paper copies.

Commission – You may get a certain percentage of each sale you make in addition to your basic salary. Really commission is a way to incentivise you to sell more, but at the end of the day, it's extra money in your pocket. Sometimes, the company may put on another incentive for the month where winning teams or individuals can receive various prizes. While I have just dangled a juicy carrot in front of you, I think it is only fair to tell you that as an apprentice in my first role, I was exempt from receiving commission and incentives.

NI – National Insurance contributions entitle you to certain benefits (for example, a state pension). It is a tax automatically deducted from your salary. Your unique National Insurance number is used by the government to record how much tax you have paid against your name.

PAYE – Stands for 'Pay As You Earn' and, like many terms on the list, it is tax related. In short, it is a system used to calculate your income tax and NI contributions via a 'PAYE code'. Your employer uses the code to work out how much you owe, deduct it from your salary, and you get the rest.

P60 – A document which outlines how much the tax you have paid over the tax year. A tax year is not from 1st January – 31st December. It is actually from 6th April – 5th April. It will be provided by your employer, and you should receive it before the 31st May each year. I recommend keeping a copy of the document somewhere safe.

P45 – A document issued by your employer when you stop working for them. It is a record of both your pay and tax deductions for the tax year. Again, keep any copies you receive in a safe place.

Probationary period – It is almost a given you will have one of these after your apprenticeship, if not during. The probationary period (usually between 3–6 months) is a time frame where the employer and you test the waters. You can both assess each other. Assuming you work hard and show your worth, you will pass the probationary period and receive the promised benefits as stated in your contract (a slight increase in pay, for example). Usually, there is a mid-term review to see if you are on track and what changes you need to make, if any. After the agreed duration, the decision will be made during the final review. Something to keep in mind, probation periods can be extended if necessary. However, the flip side is maybe they don't think you are up to scratch for whatever reason, and they can terminate your contract. The big difference; termination during a probationary period is without notice. You only receive the benefit of a notice period once you pass. The other side is in your favour. Maybe you do not think the company is the right fit for you, so you can up sticks and leave with a reduced notice period. Details regarding the length of notice you must give in relation to your length of employment should be stated in your contract.

Notice period – A set amount of time you must continue to work after you have notified the company of your resignation. As mentioned previously, you can find the specifics in your contract.

Overtime, weekends and bank holidays – As I discovered during my first apprenticeship, not all are Monday – Friday and 9 am – 5 pm. Sometimes you have to work extra on weekends or bank holidays. Usually, the company will pay you for these or give you the time back. For example, maybe you work on a Sunday and have the following Tuesday off. I can't say which you will get or how much, as the option is down to the company's discretion.

On call – I never had a job which was on call, but I imagine there are some apprenticeships (most likely medical-based) which are. On-call means you have shifts in which you must be available at any time, with little notice, during set hours. From what I understand, the intensity varies day to day, which could be a good or bad thing depending on how you want to look at it.

Expenses – Costs you can claim back from the company, provided you have the receipt for each of the purchases you have made. Each company will have their own rules on what is refundable and what isn't, but the most common costs relate to travel for work purposes. Train tickets or petrol based on mileage are the standard expenses people claim for.

SSP – If you are ill for a prolonged duration and unable to work, you will still receive money through Statutory Sick Pay (SSP). Don't take the piss with it. Companies aren't stupid; you usually have to provide a 'fit note' (issued by a doctor) as proof you were ill.

Annual leave – We all need to recharge the old batteries. Lucky for you, the company will give you a set number of days you can take off work, and still get paid. Typically, these must be booked in advance via a system and approved by your line manager. The number of days you get will be stated in your contract. In most cases, weekends don't count, so you could book off a Monday to a Monday at the cost of five days, not seven. Whether bank holidays are included is up to the organisation. My advice for annual leave, use them wisely.

Timesheet – I only had timesheets in my second apprenticeship. A timesheet is something you have to submit weekly to state where you were and what you did. Nothing too intense, but from what I gather, timesheets usually relate to financial matters, so it's in the company's interest for you to fill it out.

SSO – Again, not sure if common in other companies, but knowledge is never wasted. When you join, IT will most likely have set up all your accounts for the company systems. SSO stands for 'Single Sign On'. Rather than having various log-in details for individual platforms, one email address will be linked to all systems. Another benefit is that you only need to remember one password.

GDPR – General Data Protection Regulation. GDPR's purpose is to ensure any personal information is legitimately acquired, used, securely stored, and disposed of correctly. The company will likely ask you to complete some GDPR modules or training courses, but for valid reasons. A breach of these regulations could result in some hefty fines.

CPD – Continuous Personal Development gets thrown about a lot by employers and line managers. CPD is when you take action to develop your knowledge/skills and to remain up to date with the progression of a chosen field. CPD would be covered during your PDR.

PDR – Oh, the joys of a PDR. It stands for 'Personal Development Review'. The frequency of these varies from company to company. A PDR is when you sit with your manager to discuss your progression towards the goals stated in your last PDR. You will also cover your future goals, targets, or aspirations. They can also be used as a form of consideration when administering a pay rise.

PIP – Performance Improvement Programme. You don't want one. Being on PIP means you aren't performing to a high enough standard, and the company has decided to put a plan in place to develop your performance. I never received one, but it could be a sign of the beginning of the end if you do not change your work ethic.

Org chart – Shorthand for 'Organisational chart'. It shows where each person sits in the company hierarchy as well as the reporting relationships (usually directly, but sometimes they will show some indirect reporting lines). It is beneficial to see so you can make better sense of the team, and who some important figures in the business are.

I could keep going, but I think those are the major ones. Some may seem obvious. Others, not so much. I have no idea how knowledgeable you are, so I tried to cover all bases. Anyway, time for the last chapter.

Tip 20 – Bon Voyage

So here we are, at the end. We might as well end on a positive as the above has hardly been a selection of euphoric passages. All I have done so far is paint images of misery and suffering when it comes to apprenticeships. There's no need to tell me, I was already fully aware of the fact while writing. There is good reason for these seemingly dispiriting pages though.

I know near the beginning I mentioned my atrocious record working in sales. Regardless, to me, it's akin to a salesperson. You walk in and, once engaged in conversation and the small talk has ceased, they begin listing off the positives of whatever item has been brought into question. Why do they do it? You probably don't need the answer, but if you start a job… (Yes, I deliberately chose not to finish the dictum.)

As I'm sure you figured out, they want you to purchase the product or use the service. They aren't going to shine the spotlight on any major flaws in build quality or how the equivalent competitor is cheaper because then (shock) you are less likely to proceed with the purchase. The same goes for apprenticeship providers, job descriptions, websites and those providing advice on career days. All want you to partake in apprenticeships (whether there are personal benefits to them is another matter), so of course, these will depict a world of sunshine and rainbows.

I'm not in such a camp. As mentioned at the start, I'm not trying to sell you anything. I'm impartial to your next career choice. Plus, the book's foundation is honesty. I didn't want to write a book crammed full of the same old generic advice. I wanted to create something helpful, informative, and thought-provoking. Unfortunately for me, the generic advice around apprenticeships is usually positive, which leaves me the negatives. I'm here to tell you the truth from the perspective of somebody who has been in the apprenticeship boat twice. One of which sank.

However...

You have the option to embark on a new adventure. Perhaps you have already begun. It should have been designed so you enjoy the experience of working for the organisation. After all, they are investing time and money into you. For an organisation, the hope is that you will stay on afterwards and become a full-time employee.

You will get the opportunity to meet new people, make friends, learn a multitude of skills, and have the chance to travel or be part of events outside of work which is only possible because of the apprenticeship. You need to savour those moments while you can. Before you know it, the moment has passed, and regardless of whether you chose to participate or not, you will just be left with memories by the end of your apprenticeship.

I wish

You may have noticed I wished for a lot throughout *Apprentips*. Upon reflection, I didn't really cherish the experiences I had. I turned down many opportunities or often never gave 100 per cent to make the most of them. I was either too apprehensive, lazy or couldn't see the point. I think we can all agree just how moronic that was. I lost contact with many of the people I encountered, which is some feat considering the presence of social media. Rather than living a life of enjoyment and making the most of my teenage years and early 20s, I did the opposite. I tried the 'Five whys' technique and concluded it was because I didn't give my future genuine consideration. If I could go back in time, fuck, I'd have done so much different.

Let's be real. Those words meant absolutely nothing to you. I'm a stranger who, most likely, you have never seen, who led a life you didn't know about and is now telling you about it. So why should you care I regret numerous things?

Here's why. The entirety of what you just read includes admissions of mistakes. I also told you I was miserable at times. Furthermore, I regret a lot. Why would you want to have similar experiences too?

As I said at the beginning, what you choose to do next, whether it be an apprenticeship, gap year, university or maybe you have some other plan which is none of the previous options, makes no difference to me. However, I hope you found *Apprentips* helpful. Perhaps it even influenced your current/future decisions to some degree. Please just make sure that whatever you choose, you genuinely believe it is the right choice for you. Now go and enjoy the next stage of your life!

Maximise the opportunities presented to you, grab as many of those puzzle pieces as possible, don't be afraid of making mistakes, learn from your inevitable mistakes, create new relationships, discover your passions, start believing in yourself, challenge yourself, and make countless memories. Life is too short to waste it. It goes by in the blink of an eye, especially as an apprentice.